Light:
A Parent's Guide
for Health and
Happiness

Light:
A Parent's Guide for Health and Happiness

Dr Shelley James

DEDICATION

To my nieces, nephews and godchildren

Alice, Amity, Camille, Clara, Elea,
Gethyin, Halo, Jules, Lily, Pippa, Tomas,
Wilf, and all the other brilliant young
people in my life.

You light up my world.

CONTENTS

Preface   i

Introduction   1

1/ Rise and shine   11

2/ Walk on sunshine   39

3/ Be Brilliant   65

4/ Light and the Brain   89

5/ How lights work   113

6/ Shopping guide   124

7/ Conclusion   145

About the Author   147

Index   148

Bibliography   151

Preface

I have always wondered why we pay so little attention to the lights. You would not sit for long in a room that is too hot, or where a soundtrack is buzzing in the background without doing something about it, especially if you are trying to focus or relax. And yet light affects you just as much as heat and sound. You may be surprised to realise that light is driving every single cell in your body and brain every second of every day and has been doing so since you were just a few weeks old in the womb [1]. Light shapes how you feel and how you look. It will even affect how much of this sentence you remember [2].

But for most of us, lightbulbs are a boring everyday essential, stacked somewhere between the bleach and the toilet rolls in the household section of the store.

I didn't give lights a second thought myself until I was cycling to work one morning. I hit a patch of grease and flew over the handlebars. I landed hard, smacked my head, and broke my helmet. When I woke up, it was clear that my life would never be the same again.

The impact had scrambled the switches between my eye and brain: my sensitivity to light was off the scale.

People who live in dread of crippling migraines will know what I mean. A simple meeting felt as overwhelming as a complex negotiation in a nightclub with jetlag and 'the flu: stressful and painful. I was constantly on the verge of tears. It was tempting to draw the curtains and disconnect from the world.

But I was lucky to have a brilliant team around me, including a neurologist. So I learnt to retrain all those switches one by one through long, dark years. I set up a residency at the Eye Hospital. I took a PhD. I even trained as an electrician. I became fascinated by just how powerful light is. In particular, I learned how light makes your body clock tick [3].

We're only just beginning to understand how this remarkable system works. But we do know that before the alarm clock went off this morning, your body clock had bumped up your blood pressure, core temperature, and even the thickness of your blood so that you were ready to get up [4]. By noon, it will have boosted your metabolism, working memory and muscle tone to get you pumped up and set to take a giant step for the team [5].

And as night falls, your body clock will get ready to flip the incoming data stream through the silent hours of the night. You may think you are resting, but the brain is hard at work reviewing the activities from the day, logging the memories you need, clearing out the rubbish, and flooding your body and brain with growth and repair hormones [6].

Parallel pathways

Scientists only recently discovered this parallel pathway from the eye to the central pacemaker. This tiny gland is tucked safely in the centre of your brain, protected by your skull - and hopefully by your cycle helmet. It's dark in there. So the only way your body clock can tell what time it is in the outside world and what to do next is by interpreting signals from your senses. Those signals might be food or physical exercise. But the single most reliable and universal sign we share with every living organism, from plants to plankton, is the thousand-fold difference between bright days under the sun and dark nights in shimmering moonlight.

When your central pacemaker doesn't know what's happening, either because the difference between day and night isn't clear enough or because those signals arrive in a random sequence, the system starts to break down. If you've ever crossed time zones or worked a night shift, you might have tasted that disorientation. You might struggle to focus and crave comfort food at odd times during the night. You might be surprised to know that taking to the wheel after just 17 hours without sleep is the equivalent of driving under the influence of alcohol.

Silent killer

Most of us will soon recover from short-term disruption. But over time, not getting enough sleep can be literally a killer. For example, data from a recent study that followed almost 7,000 Britains over 25 years showed that people who enjoy less than five hours of sleep per night at the age of 50, 60, and 70 was linked to a 30% to 40% increased risk of suffering from multiple health conditions when compared with those who slept for up to seven hours compared to those who got seven hours per night. Getting five hours or less at age 50 was associated with 25% increased risk of mortality over the 25 years of follow-up [7].

The World Health Organisation classified disrupting your body clock as a probable carcinogen back in 2007 [8], a decade before long-term studies revealed just how deadly the wrong light at the wrong time can be.

Your body clock is marvellously patient and forgiving and will run happily in the background if you give it the information it needs.

But the homes where we spend 90% of our lives don't give our body clock the bright-dark contrast it desperately needs. During the day, the average living room or office is a fraction of the light levels outside. In the evening, most living rooms are hundreds of times brighter than natural dusk. To make matters worse, we extend our synthetic diet of light into the midnight hours [9]: 42% of Brits people sleep with a light on [10]because we're scared of the dark. One in three young people checks their phones at least once in the night, firing up their body clocks with bright blue light and social interaction [11] [12].

Most of us can reset our body clocks if we get outside more and switch off after dark. But one in three people living in long-term residential care in America may not take a breath of fresh air outside this month at all. One in five American children may not go out to play today [13]. That may sound extreme. But most adults do little better. Americans spend, on average, less than an hour a day outside [14], with 44% of 18-24 year olds getting outside for less than 30 minutes per day [15]. That is less than the United Nations minimum for somebody living in prison [16].

Lessons in lockdown

Through the lockdowns during the Covid-19 pandemic, I saw my beautiful nieces and wonderful goddaughter locked inside. Perhaps you were there too, with the curtains drawn, trying to learn online during the day and trying to make friends on social media at night. I saw their body clocks start to break down. I was desperately worried because I knew how vital those transition years were for their future health and happiness.

I spoke to them about light and whether they felt it might help: I knew from personal experience that it could. But they rolled their eyes: 'No, they don't learn about that stuff at school. It's boring anyway.' I spoke to their parents, who had no idea either.

I was sure that someone had thought of this before. So I started to search online and came across NASA's Space Programme. I learnt about their billion-dollar research to optimise the lighting for the space station. But, of course, this investment makes perfect sense: those astronauts are locked down in a small room and always online. They certainly don't get out much, and as they zoom around the moon, they see 16 sunrises for every one of ours.

Rocket scientists and down-to-earth solutions

Remarkably, the scientists who work on the Space Programme responded to my emails: thanks to the pandemic, they weren't jetting off to conferences. They patiently explained the emerging science of light and the body clock. They generously introduced me to manufacturers building new systems based on their discoveries. These industry leaders introduced me to their clients: pioneering business people with a passion for the health and happiness of their teams who were harnessing these innovations to create healthier, happier spaces too.

I spoke to the clinical director of a neonatal unit who invested in a state-of-the-art lighting system for his patients, premature babies fighting for their lives. He spoke passionately about new hope for these fragile lives and their families and the pride of watching them grow and thrive[17]. I talked to the facilities manager of a school for children with hearing loss. These young students could finally lip-read more efficiently and communicate at last [18]. I interviewed an industrialist in Norway: his teams were so delighted with the lighting in the office that they invited their friends and family to visit with pride [19]. Finally, I spent a day with the chief executive of an award-winning Elderly Care home in Warwickshire. He convinced his Board to invest in lighting to reduce the distressing agitation that affects people with dementia at about five o'clock in the evening. The results have been overwhelmingly positive for staff and residents alike. They are steadily extending the approach across the Trust [20].

So I knew that lighting made a difference. And I knew there was something I could do about it and that I was not alone.

2.5 million teens in four months

I went back to the scientists and manufacturers to ask for help checking the science and sponsorship to cover costs. Bristol University generously hosted focus groups with teens to get the content and the style right. My brother, who leads an international PR agency, gave me practical advice and endless encouragement. And my mother patiently donated her spare room and perfected the recipe for homemade bread while I recorded and edited for days on end through that long lockdown summer.

Together we set up a social media campaign for teens about how light could help them. These 30-second video clips have reached over two and a half million teens so far. It's always profoundly humbling when a teenager from across the planet reaches out to let me know that they're drawing the curtains in the morning, that they've been outside - and that they've even taken their grumpy old parents with them too.

Those teens told me the advice was useful - and that it made a difference. Then they pointed out that don't buy the lights.

I soon realised they were right.

Most professionals who specify lighting have little or no training on how their decisions affect the health and well-being of all of us who spend our lives in their buildings. They work to tight deadlines and even tighter budgets. So not surprisingly, they buy on price to meet the minimum legal standard. Their clients naturally follow the professionals' advice. The manufacturers complain that there is no demand for a higher specification, and the value chain is locked into a box-ticking exercise.

Talking to the grown-ups

So I set out to do something about that too. I created a social media campaign for businesses. The International WELL Building Institute invited me to serve on their Advisory Panel and Faculty. I lead workshops and present at conferences around the world. I helped to set up a PhD with Oxford University and host debates between scientists, manufacturers and Care Providers, Education Trusts and Housing Associations.

My clients often work for global brands. But they are all mums and dads, sisters and sons too. They all ask the same questions: how can light help the people they love to wake up feeling refreshed and energised, feel happier and confident in their ability to learn?

They often ask where they can find out more.

So I wrote this book.

It is a work in progress: new information is coming to light every day, and it is my first attempt at writing something like this.

But if you have started to think a bit more about the humble lightbulbs all around you and even make some small changes yourself, this book will have done its job.

Introduction

As a parent, you will do everything in your power to give your family the best start in life. You lie awake worrying when they seem tired and struggle to get out of bed. You are constantly looking for ways to help them cope with depression and anxiety as they wrestle with overwhelming pressure online and at school. You invest everything you have to give them the best education you can afford, knowing that a love of learning holds the key to their future success and happiness.

You may be surprised to learn that simple changes to their diet of light will make a world of difference to their sleep, mood and academic performance too [21]. A growing body of evidence suggests that these natural remedies can be better than antidepressants or sleep medication and boost their academic results by up to 25% [22].

You will discover proven practical tips and 'killer arguments' to share with the young people in your life to encourage them to make healthier choices for themselves. You will learn about the recent discovery of an entirely new class of cells in the eye that revolutionised the lighting on the space station and laid the foundations for the next generation of affordable, sustainable lighting solutions down here on Earth. Finally, you will learn what to look for when shopping for lights so you can provide a healthy, happy home- and save money too.

Just as an apple is not a healthy diet on its own, the humble lightbulb will not transform your life overnight. But it is a brilliant place to start.

What's so special about light?

Before we begin, I invite you to take a moment to picture your fondest memories. The atmosphere, whether cosy firelight, a glowing sunset or bright summer sunshine, is a vital part of that golden image in your mind's eye.

That's not surprising. People have been captivated by light since the beginning of time and every civilisation celebrates its power. Let me take you on a brief journey through time to uncover the key moments in the history of the study of light and explore the festivals that have celebrated its brilliance.

In the earliest days of human history, our ancestors looked up at the sky and marvelled at the sun and the stars. The ancient Egyptians, for example, worshipped the sun god Ra and held festivals to honour him around 3,000 BCE. In India, the festival of Diwali, the "Festival of Lights," dates back thousands of years and is still celebrated today. It signifies the victory of light over darkness and good over evil. The Chinese Lantern Festival, held on the 15th day of the first lunar month, celebrates the return of light after the darkness of winter. In the Jewish tradition, the eight-day festival of Hanukkah, or the "Festival of Lights," commemorates the miracle of a single day's supply of oil lasting for eight days during the rededication of the Second Temple in Jerusalem.

Light and sight

Philosophers, including Empedocles and later Plato and Aristotle, pondered the nature of light. They believed that sight and light were so intimately connected that vision was a sign of life itself. Dancing 'crystalline spirits' lived inside the eye - just behind the coloured ring called the iris. These ambassadors of the soul went out into the world to bring information back to the intellect. This is their way of explaining the way that some people see to be able to see things that others cannot. If you have ever lost your keys and found them hiding in plain sight, you will know what they meant.

In the 10th century, the Arab scholar Alhazen turned this human-centred theory on its head with his groundbreaking work, "The Book of Optics." He realised that light existed even when there were no eyes to see it. His discoveries laid the foundation for modern optics, as his calculations described the way that rays of light travel through space and materials. He was also the first to describe how the eye perceives light accurately.

But his work was not translated for centuries, so the ancient theories of 'eye beames' persisted until the revolution in science and art that became known as the Enlightenment in the 17th century. The British polymath Isaac Newton and Christiaan Huygens engaged in a heated debate about the nature of light. Newton maintained that light was made of particles, or "corpuscles," while Huygens believed that it was a wave.

This argument seemed to have been settled in 1801 when Thomas Young performed his famous double-slit experiment. He showed a beam of light moving, like water passing through a gap in a wall, to create ripples or waves with peaks and troughs. But this left as many questions as it answered: centuries of scientific research, including Alhazen and Newton, had clearly demonstrated that rays could be directed like a stream of particles.

It wasn't until the early 20th century that Albert Einstein's work on the photoelectric effect helped to reconcile these two. He showed that light could be both a particle and a wave, depending on how it was observed. This duality was further supported by the development of quantum mechanics in the 1920s and 1930s. This understanding laid the foundation for everyday technologies, including the humble lightbulb, as we will see later in the book.

Light and health

Our fascination with the healing power of light has an equally fascinating history. The Greek physician Hippocrates was fascinated that patients who were exposed to sunlight seemed to recover more quickly than those who were not. He even built a solarium at his treatment centre on the Greek island of Kos [23], while fellow physician, Aretaeus of Cappadocia is famously quoted as saying "Lethargics are to be laid in the light, and exposed to the rays of the sun for the disease is gloom." [24]

Hippocrates noticed that certain colours of light seemed to have different effects on the body - red light, for example, seemed to increase circulation, while blue light had a calming effect.

Eastern traditions take a similar approach: Ayurvedic healers believe that the body is composed of different types of energy, or doshas and that these energies can be balanced through exposure to different colours of light. For example, red light is thought to stimulate the body's energy flow, while blue light tends to be cooling and can help reduce inflammation. [25]

Traditional Chinese Medicine (TCM) also recognises the importance of light in healing. TCM practitioners use a technique called acupoint phototherapy, which involves shining specific colours of light onto specific points on the body to promote balance and healing. In TCM, each colour of light is associated with a different organ system and is used to treat specific conditions [26].

More recently, Florence Nightingale would position patients close to windows, arguing that *'second only to their need of fresh air is their need for light ... not only light but direct sun-light'*. In the early 20th century, Niels Finsen developed light therapy for the treatment of skin tuberculosis, and Robert Koch showed that the bacterium responsible for TB could be killed by sunlight. There followed a fashion for heliotherapy, until the rise of critical voices such as those of the British surgeon John Lockhart-Mummery, who, in his book *Nothing New Under the Sun,* dismissed sunlight therapy as 'pseudo-magic'. Linda Geddes' book, Chasing the Sun offers a more nuanced view of of our changing understanding of the impact of light on health [27]

Value

Any keen gardener - or window box amateur will know just how much light and shade matter to the health of your plants. A wine-lover may seek out a vintage from an exceptionally sunny year or a vineyard with a favourable orientation. You may not be surprised to learn that the price of land is linked to sunshine as much as to water.

Estate agents are equally aware of our fascination with daylight. Every listing is likely to include the words 'bright' or 'sunny'. If you look carefully at the photos, the most appealing ones are likely to be taken with all the lights switched on, even in daylight and be shot on a sunny day. A recent study of home values in San Diego found that those facing either southeast or northeast have a premium of about 12.8% and 9.6%, respectively compared to other orientations because of the way they catch the morning light without the glare of full southern exposure. [28]

The traces of our intuitive understanding of the power of this life force are in your DNA and drive every decision you make, even when you are completely blind to its effects.

You are already an expert. Now it's time how to take control of your diet of light for health and happiness.

How to use this book

This book is designed as a practical introduction to how light can help to solve the most pressing problems hundreds of parents have asked me about: how can they help their children to sleep better, to feel happier, especially during the winter months, and get the best results they can at school. These are all linked, of course: they will feel down if they aren't sleeping - and will find it even harder to get on with their homework if they feel tired and unhappy.

But the mechanisms and the solutions are slightly different. So I've structured the main chapters to focus on these three topics.

Each chapter kicks off with a quick, 'how it works' section about the underlying process. Then, a 'what you can do' set of practical tips followed by a 'what about?' section that covers some of the questions I am asked most often. Finally, I've chosen some key facts or 'killer arguments' to share with the young people in your life. The aim is to give them the information they need to make better decisions for themselves. This selection is based on the feedback I've had from teens - I'd love to know which ones your family found most compelling - and what else yo'd like to know.

I've put two more technical chapters at the end if you want to dive into them: how your child's eye and brain develop, how different kinds of lighting work and a simple shopping guide. I've also linked them to a QR code if you prefer to go online directly.

My goal is for you to get the tips you need during your lunch break, on your commute home or while you wait to collect the kids from an after school club.

I hope you enjoy reading this book as much as I have enjoyed putting it together.

1/ Rise and shine

"Everything you do, you'll do better with a good night's sleep."

Arianna Huffington

Author and founder,

The Huffington Post

Introduction

As a parent, you worry about your children getting enough rest. You know that a good night's sleep will help them to grow fit and healthy, to manage their emotions and concentrate at school.

You are right to take sleep seriously. Recent research confirms that a lack of sleep and disruption to the body clock is the single most significant factor in your life expectancy and risk of suffering from multiple physical and mental health conditions in your middle and later years. [29]

The World Health Organisation confirms that disruption to your circadian rhythm is a probable carcinogen.[30]

And yet, making sure they get the sleep they desperately need can be a daily battle. Some children are afraid of the dark and struggle with nightmares, while teens can spend all night online and hardly get up at all over the weekend. You may have trouble relaxing too. Feeling exhausted can make it even harder to concentrate at work and be calm and present as you know you should. Sleep difficulties tend to run in families, so you may feel anxious and depressed and believe that you will never be able to wake up feeling refreshed.

You may have cut down on caffeine and sugar because they can make switching off harder. You may also steer clear of alcohol during the week because you know you will struggle to sleep through the night. You may even take sleep medication, invest in a meditation or sleep-tracking app or use one of the hundreds of herbal remedies you will find on every health store shelf.

These solutions can all offer short term relief. But there is one piece of the puzzle that you may be sleepwalking past right now. And that's light.

The right light at the right time can improve the quality and quantity of sleep at any age. So even if you come from a family of light sleepers and have wrestled with insomnia for years, it is not too late to give your body clock a helping hand.

"Sleep is an investment in the energy you need to be effective tomorrow."

Tim Roth
English Director and Actor

Why do you feel sleepy?

How tired you feel is driven by two complementary systems.

1/Sleep pressure

The first driver is how long you've been awake. This natural drowsiness is known as 'sleep pressure'. You can override this feeling if you need to. But then your need to sleep catches up with you, and you suddenly feel exhausted.

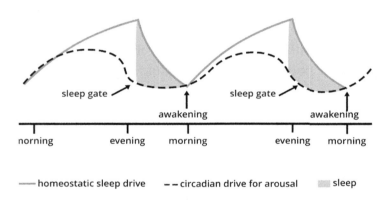

Sleep pressure

While you sleep, those hormone levels slowly settle back to normal - like taking a plug out of a bath. If you drink coffee late in the afternoon or take a long nap close to bedtime, you release that pressure too soon.

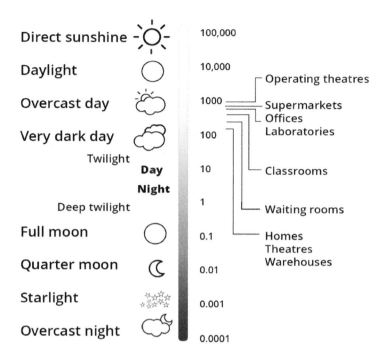

Differences in light levels outside and indoors

Alcohol has a similar effect. You're more likely to wake up in the middle of the night and struggle to get back to sleep. This is known as a 'sleep gate'.

Everyone needs different amounts of sleep, and some people find it easier to handle coffee and alcohol than others. But allowing that sleep pressure to build up during the day will help you to sleep soundly through the night. hat doesn't mean all naps are bad news. A short rest of as little as nine minutes, but ideally no more than 20 minutes immediately after lunch, can be a valuable reset for children and adults alike. The benefits are even greater if you follow that down-time with a short walk outside in daylight. You can improve your mood, consolidate memories and feel more alert. One study among sleep-deprived college students found that a brief nap, followed by a short period of bright cool light, was better than a cup of coffee.[31]

2/ Body clock

The second drive for sleep is known as your body clock or 'circadian' cycle (circa = around, dian = day).

That day-night cycle is driven by light. Or more precisely, by the massive difference in light levels between day and night.

Special cells in the eye evolved to respond to bright light, especially fresh sky blue light from the sky and across the horizon.

They send signals directly to a tiny structure known as the central pacemaker, tucked deep in the hypothalamus at the top of the brain stem. The pacemaker is like a master chef that coordinates every other system in your body. Melatonin is one of the hormones the central pacemaker uses to tell your body clock that it's dark and safe to wind down.

When the sun comes up, levels of melatonin fall and cortisol rise.

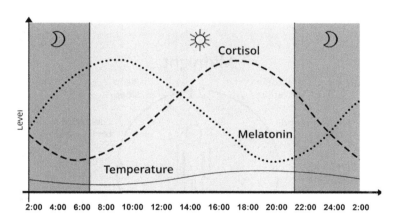

Melatonin and Cortisol cycles

The problem is that most places where we spend 90% of our time are not bright enough to give your body clock the 'wake up' signal it's seeking. Most of our homes and offices are much too bright at night, so it never gets dark enough to tell your brain that it's safe to switch off. This 'always on' feeling is made worse because your brain can't distinguish between the blue wavelengths that most computer screens and indoor lights generate and natural light from the sun and moon. One recent report found that the average home was bright enough in the evening to suppress the healthy evening rise in melatonin in half of the population. Worryingly, the paper also notes that those of us who light our homes with energy-efficient LED lightbulbs are at especially high risk for reasons we'll discover later in the book. [32]

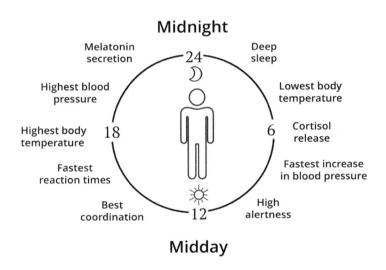

Circadian cycle

Your body clock gets even more confused because we often eat, exercise or check social media and emails late at night. Just like a toddler, you will try to stay awake in case something exciting is about to happen - good or bad. And just like that toddler, if you wind down at the same time every day and create a calm, peaceful space without distractions, you will eventually drop off to sleep.

How much sleep do you need?

There are government guidelines about how much sleep you need based on average health, age and other variables that we know make a difference, like weather and exercise. So these figures are a guide rather than a rule, just like a recommended calorie or step count. But it's a good place to start.

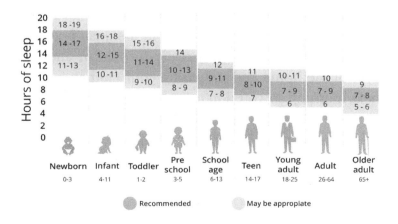

Recommended sleep for different ages

What's your chronotype?

Everyone naturally prefers to go to bed and wake up at slightly different times. That makes sense when you think of our origins living as a tribe out in the wild: you want some people to be awake early and others to keep watch at night.

Scientists have grouped these basic preferences into four types or patterns known as "chronotypes' that reflect our preferred sleep-wake pattern. You may feel strongly that one description fits you more than another. But preferences change with age, and some people are more flexible than others. You may have noticed this when travelling long haul: some people still feel unsettled after a week, while others seem to slot into the new time zone overnight.

Understanding that everyone is unique and learning about your own personal style can help you to organise daily routines so everyone can get the rest they need. For example, if your partner is awake before dawn and you're happiest in the quiet hours of the night, consider getting ready for bed in another part of the home and preparing your clothes for the next morning so you don't disturb each other during the week. You could think of this like having different diets: one may be a vegetarian while the other may love meat. During the week, you might eat separate meals, then choose a menu together for a weekend or special occasion.

Charismatic lions

 15% of the population

 Traits
Natural leaders, charismatic,
early risers

 Productivity tip
Know when it's time to switch off, take
time for yourself at the end of the day

 Celebrity lion
Richard Branson
Founder, Virgin Group

6 - 7 AM	Wake up		**4 - 9 PM**	Relax and unwind
8 AM - 12 PM	Focus on deep work		**9 -10 PM**	Get ready for bed
12 - 4 PM	Work on lighter tasks		**10 PM - 6 AM**	Sleep

Easy-going bears

 55% of the population

 Traits
Happy-go-lucky, continuous flow of
mellow energy, extroverted

 Productivity tip
Schedule meetings in the morning and
try to finish up before late afternoon

 Celebrity bear
Oprah Winfrey
Founder, OWN

7 - 8 AM	Wake up		**4 - 10 PM**	Relax and unwind
10 AM - 2 PM	Focus on deep work		**10 - 11 PM**	Get ready for bed
2 - 4 PM	Work on lighter tasks		**11 PM - 7AM**	Sleep

Creative Wolves

 15% of the population

 Traits
Introspective, highly creative and introverted

 Productivity tip
Get ahead on work at home while you're feeling most awake

 Celebrity wolf
Alex Ohanian
Co-Founder, Reddit

7:30 - 9 AM	Wake up		**5 - 9 PM**	Engage in creative tasks
10 AM - 12 AM	Focus on lighter tasks		**9 -10 PM**	Unwind from the day
12 - 2 PM	Complete deep or creative work		**10 PM - 12 AM**	Prepare for bed
2 - 5 PM	Focus on lighter less intense tasks		**12 - 7:30 AM**	Sleep

Brainy dolphins

 10% of the population

 Traits
Highly intelligent. Scatterbrained, with bursts of creative energy

 Productivity tip
If needed, take breaks throughout the day to mentally reset and recharge

 Celebrity dolphin
Jackson Pollock
Artist

6:30 - 7:30	Wake up		**4 - 10 PM**	Relax, unwind from the day
8 - 10 AM	Focus on lighter tasks		**10 - 11:30 PM**	Prepare for bed
10 AM - 12 PM	Complete deep or creative work		**12 - 6:30 AM**	Sleep
12 - 4 PM	Focus on lighter less intense tasks			

What you can do...

Here are proven, practical ways to optimise your exposure to natural and artificial light during the day and and darkness at night to improve sleep.

One useful metaphor is to see your body clock like a child on a swing: you know that it takes time to build up momentum but once it's moving happily, you can give it a gentle push at the end of the arc and it will keep going smoothly. Equally, if you try to stop it mid-swing, the rhythm is broken - that sudden interruption can even be dangerous.

Help your body clock plan ahead

Simple changes to lighting - brightness and colour, for example - will create a series of clear signals for the body and brain that something is about to happen. For example, you can open the curtains or switch from bright cool overhead lighting to low-level warm lights to let small children know that it's time to get up, snuggle down to read or get ready for bed. You can use colour-changing light strips to create a playful space or a quiet camp. Children who suffer from anxiety or are on the autistic spectrum can find these techniques especially useful because it helps them to predict what is going to happen next and avoid surprises which they can find stressful.

With older children and teens, you can set a regular schedule at home using changes in the lighting. These signals will help them settle down in structured, focused study sessions, just as they would in the classroom.

In the evening, a shift to different lighting - coloured LEDs or softer table lamps, for example - will help them to wind down to socialise and relax, revise the lessons for the day and then go to sleep. This clear difference between work and rest is a vital life skill that will help them to set boundaries, make time for self-care and cope with pressures in later life.

Get back to basics

1/ Bright light = rise and shine

 Bright light in the morning is the most powerful and reliable signal that it's time to be awake. So encouraging the young people in your life to get outside for thirty minutes of daylight before 9 am will improve their quality and quantity of sleep at night. This wake-up signal is the equivalent of eating a balanced and protein-rich breakfast to set your metabolism up for the day. That's because early morning light has a high proportion of

those 'sky blue' wavelengths that the body clock recognises as a 'wake up' signal.

Taking another short break in daylight at lunchtime can be more effective than a cup of coffee to boost your energy levels and concentration.

Sitting close to a window during the day will make a big difference too. Your position in the room is critical because the light levels fall rapidly as you move away from the source: your eyes might be enjoying as much as 3,000 units of light or lux next to the window and just 100 in the middle of the room.

Position your chair at right angles if you can. This way, you will make the most of every ray of sunlight. The movement of the sun across the sky and shifting weather also create the experience of hundreds of small 'events' that contribute to sleep pressure. At the same time, you will avoid the problems of glare and contrast that can arise when facing a window directly or when you have your back to it.

Late afternoon is a great time to get out into natural daylight again. You could make a call, listen to messages, or review progress on your 'to-do' list for the day. That's because the percentage of those wake-up sky-blue wavelengths goes up again as the sun gets lower in the sky. These three 30-minute breaks will help your body clock to tell the time and set a solid foundation for a good night's sleep.

2/ Campfire glow = wind down

 Like a strong coffee, bright 'blue' light stays in the system for around two hours. So switch the lights to be as soft and dim as possible. In the summer, this may mean drawing the curtains, especially for children who are especially sensitive to evening light. This clear and regular contrast will show your body clock that it's safe to shift gears and prepare for a good night's sleep.

As the sun sets, levels of the hormone melatonin naturally rise as cortisol levels fade. Eating early and enjoying relaxing exercise, reviewing events of the day with friends and family or listening to music or podcasts are all part of a healthy bedtime routine.

But the body clock is also alert to other signs indicating the need to be awake. Socialising, exercise that raises the heart rate and temperature, and the prospect of a meal can create conflict and destabilise that critical cycle. Our exposure to blue light in the evening comes from screens and phones because we watch films and check social media. As a result, you compound the alerting effect of the unnatural light with those other wake-up cues.

So the first step is to cut light levels to a soft glow and switch off screens and notifications that are hard to resist. Then use the relaxing effect of colour temperature to prepare the brain for sleep. Just as you can create the 'fresh air' feeling with cool light during the day, you can generate a cosy 'campfire' glow atmosphere to help your little ones wind down and prepare for sleep.

Blue filters and timed shifts in screen brightness and colour are promoted as ways to reduce exposure to the 'wake-up' wavelengths. However, there is very little scientific research that proves that they effectively support the melatonin cycle. That's for two reasons: the first is that, as we've seen, the specialist cells that send signals to the body clock are a relay station for all the other light-sensing cells too. So they will only come into their own when the light levels are very low indeed. Also, no amount of light filtering will fix the underlying problem that if you are on screen you are probably online - a powerful signal to your brain that there are other people around and you need to be awake to connect with them.

3/ Darkness = switch off

Complete darkness to sleep at night is just as important as the bright morning light: the faintest sound or glimmer of light is enough to keep us from falling into the deepest stages critical to physical and mental health.

Sleeping with the equivalent of a standard light bulb in an overhead light for one night can increase your risk of depression. As a rough guide, it's too bright if you can see your feet at the end of the bed. In addition, one study found that people who read a book using an electronic reading device before sleep took two hours longer the next day to feel fully awake compared to those who read a printed book.

Light indoors is one of many issues that get in the way of a good night's sleep. The glow from street lamps and passing traffic are equally disruptive. People who live in urban areas with high levels of light pollution are at increased risk of premature births, depression in teenagers and the prevalence of Parkinson's in older adults.[33]

So make sure the bedrooms are dark: black-out curtains are the most effective solution, but if that's not an option, use an eye mask and charge your phone and screens outside the bedroom. Even the glow from standby lights and electric alarm clocks will be enough to stop your brain from switching off and leave you feeling groggy the following day. Switching off will cut your electricity bill too.

What about...

Here are answers to some of the questions that people ask me most often.

Teens who sleep into the afternoon?

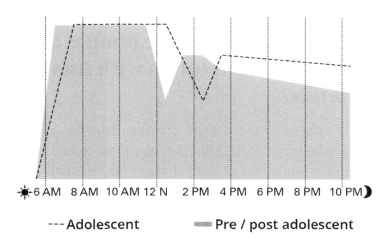

---Adolescent   ▬ Pre / post adolescent

Teen circadian cycle shift

A teenager's body clock runs two hours later than an adult's. So they naturally go to bed later and struggle to wake up.

Luckily, even in the afternoon, the light is still many times brighter outside than indoors. So getting outside, whenever you can encourage them to do so, will help to give their body clock a clear difference between daytime and night.

Afternoon sunlight can even be better for people with fair skin because there are fewer UVB wavelengths in daylight in the afternoon. Even if they check social media and chat with friends online, time outside will give them a little exercise and some fresh air. These will all be signals to help to get their body clock back on track.

Teens who need their phones at night to stay in touch with their friends?

The pressure to stay connected is almost overwhelming for adults, let alone for teens. Their teenage years are a critical time for them to build social networks and develop their own separate identity as adults. You were probably the same. That inevitably means testing the boundaries with you as a parent, which can be exhausting and demoralising. But you know how important it is for them to learn to trust their own judgement, separate from their peers so that they can pursue their own goals in life. That means setting clear limits for them about screen time so they can get the rest they so desperately need.

One solution is to negotiate different rules between weekdays and weekends. One study showed that students with parent-enforced bedtimes got more sleep than those who were allowed to set their own [34]. They may not thank you for it at the time, but this is definitely a battle worth fighting: they can always tell their friends it's your fault!

Children who are afraid of the dark?

Young children often experience vivid dreams and nightmares. These can be a natural way for their brains to process information from the day. Unfortunately, this can mean they are scared of going to sleep and want to leave the lights on. The problem is that their brains do not get the deep rest they need to help them manage these strong emotions. These fears and habits continue into their teenage years and lead to a cycle of chronic sleep deprivation[35].

So it is essential to take the time to help young children to manage their natural fear of the unknown and set up healthy bedtime routines that will serve them into adulthood and old age. The first step is acknowledging and validating your child's fear of the dark. Avoid dismissing their feelings or telling them there is nothing to fear. Instead, listen to their concerns and offer reassurance that you are there to help them feel safe.

A simple routine that involves reading or quiet play and time to review their favourite moments from the day will create a positive atmosphere. A calm and comforting sleep environment can also help. Amber-coloured night lights in their room and the hallway will offer the reassurance they need.

Children who can't get back to sleep?

The cycle of anxiety about not being able to sleep can become part of the problem. The science shows that simply believing you have had enough sleep can be enough to boost mood and performance, in the short term at least.

If they're worried about something, encourage them to write down their concerns before bedtime to 'park' them: the Latin American tradition of handing over your concerns to worry dolls can be a soothing remedy for younger children.

The simple practice of free writing - taking 15 minutes to 'download' your feelings and worries onto the page has been shown to reduce stress in adults.[36]

Set up a soft, comforting bedside lamp light they can switch on if they find themselves lying awake. A soothing soundtrack will also help.

'Killer arguments'

I know first-hand that young people may not want to take advice from adults, however well-meaning we may be. So here are some facts that might help them to take their sleep seriously and make decisions about light that will help them to rise and shine

What's sleep good for?

Students who regularly get enough sleep...

O Get better results at school: earlier and more regular bed times and longer average sleep times boost academic performance by up to 25% [37].

O Fight off infections and recover more quickly from sports injuries: one study found that athletes who had less than 8 hours per night had a 1.7 times greater risk of injury and took longer to recover. Another found reduced resistance to infectious diseases like COVID-19 which meant they could't train or compete [38].

O Manage mood swings and stressful situations better: Compared to a normal nights' sleep, just one night without going to bed can make the instant emotion response part of your brain (the amygdala) 60% more likely to react to negative pictures[39].

What's light got to do with it?

○ Your body clock needs a clear signal that it's safe to go into deep sleep. Darkness is the main signal it uses to release the hormone melatonin. These hormones take a while to kick in: it takes around around two hours for the 'wake up' signals to wear off - like a coffee [40].

○ Blue light from your screen in the evening tricks your body clock into believing you still need to be awake. Your eyes can still sense light even when your eyelids are closed so even a little bit of light stops your brain going into the best kind of deep sleep [41].

○ Lying in bed with the curtains closed stops your body clock getting the 'wake-up' signals it needs to release energising hormones including cortisol. If you give your body clock a solid signal in the morning, it is more forgiving if you stay up a bit later in the evening. [42]

So what can you do?

○ Switch off screens at least two hours before bed to give your body clock time to wind down.

○ Make sure it's dark in your room. That means asking for some black-out curtains or blinds or wearing an eye mask and switching off notifications and 'standby' indicators on screens, digital alarms and other electronics.

O Give your body clock a clear wake-up signal by giving it a blast of bright, cool light as soon as you wake up. During the winter months, you might be awake long before the sun comes up. So switch on the lights if you want to feel alert and get outside as soon as the sun comes up. That's because because it's much brighter outside than it is indoors even on a cloudy day. First thing in the morning is but any time will do! Standing on a balcony or by an open window is better than nothing - glass cuts out lots of the wavelengths your body clock needs.

Conclusion

We all want to look forward to a good night's sleep and wake up refreshed and ready to tackle whatever the day might hold. As a parent, you know how much happier and more relaxed your children are when they're rested. You might lie awake worrying about the amount of time your teens spend online at night and try everything you can to get them to switch off.

But you might be missing out on the simplest, most reliable and sustainable solution of them all, hiding in plain sight: the right light at the right time. Encourage them to get outside, ideally, every morning before 10 am, give them a regular bedtime routine and let them know just how much better they will feel - and how much better their results will be - if they draw the curtains, switch off and rest.

If you start these habits early, they will find it easier to handle the social and academic pressures of teenage years and their changing body clocks If you set an example, they are more likely to follow your advice. Light won't guarantee a great night's sleep every time. But it will give your body clock a helping hand.

"Sleep is the single most effective thing we can do to reset our brain and body health each day."

Matthew Walker, Centre for Human Sleep Science at the University of California, Berkeley

Checklist for better sleep

1. Do your family members know why sleep matters and how it can help them to do the things they want to do?

2. Do you have a regular morning and bedtime routine that you all follow every day including weekends and holidays?

3. Is the lighting in your home set up to help you all to get a good nights' sleep?

   O Bright enough during the day?

   O Dim and warm in the evening?

   O Dark at night?

Further reading

I've put links and academic papers online so it's easier for you to track them down. I can check and update them more easily too. Please use this QR cod.e

2/ Walk on sunshine

"Here comes the sun!"

The Beatles

Introduction

How can light help us feel happier is the question I get asked the most. Parents, especially, worry when their children struggle with depression, knowing that they are missing precious moments of discovery and freedom that will never come again.

Parents and teachers are all too aware that good mental health is key to being able to concentrate, learn, and make friends at school. We know that when young people feel balanced and self-assured, they find it easier to share their feelings, negotiate, and sort out conflicts calmly. We know that feeling positive is critical to healthier choices and keeping a perspective through the dark times that everyone goes through.

Every caring adult will do everything in their power to give these growing bodies and minds the best start in life: the average parent in the UK invests up to 20% of their salary on after-school activities, holidays and specialist equipment.

And yet, unless a young person is formally diagnosed with a specific condition, most of us don't make the connection between light and mental health.

Perhaps it's time we did.

There's growing evidence that spending just 30 minutes in bright light can be as effective as antidepressants without the harmful side effects or long-term dependency these medications can bring[43].

The next generation of 'SAD' and dawn simulator lamps can complement daylight and deliver the active ingredients our mood-regulating system needs. Lighting can help in other ways, too, from reducing stress through a sense of personal control to reminding us of happier times and offering fresh perspectives.

This chapter will explain how you can harness this powerful natural high so you, your family and friends can see the silver lining, even in the darkest days.

"The mind, like the body, can be moved from the shade into sunshine."

Andrew Carnegie

Scottish-American industrialist and philanthropist

Why do you feel happy?

Why are some people born smiling, while others seem to struggle to see the bright side of life from the moment they come into the world?

Of course, life has its ups and downs. Many face desperate challenges, from family breakdown, academic pressure and financial worries to physical disabilities and natural disasters. And yet, even those who, from the outside at least, seem blessed with a golden life and a bright future on the horizon can experience crippling anxiety and depression, especially through their teenage years.

As a parent who has known your child since birth, you may not be surprised that around half of their natural tendency to smile is genetic. That means that there is at least half of the happiness equation that you can do something about!

Light affects your mood in three fundamental ways. The first is regulating the body clock, as the previous chapter shows. But not only does the right light at the right time help you to sleep, but it also helps to shift your emotional state, particularly early in the morning when your mood tends to be at its lowest ebb. This state shift can be a game-changer for teens and mums going through hormone changes after pregnancy or into menopause. The second is the way that bright light gives a natural boost to the hormone-regulating systems that can get out of balance across a range of mood disorders, from depression to bipolar disorder. The third is simply the power of light to create a comfortable and uplifting environment where everyone can feel valued and safe. Studies of burnout show that a sense of control and respect can be as critical as the workload itself. *

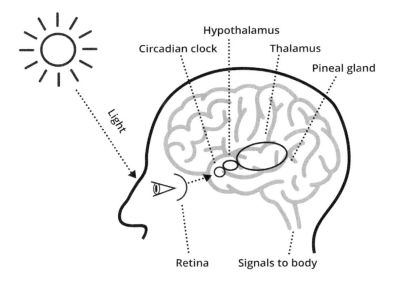

Light and mood connection

So many classic songs and sayings remind us of the link between light and happiness, from 'feeling gloomy' to 'seeing the light' and being a 'ray of sunshine'. A new generation of scientists are working out exactly how light helps us to feel bright. Their experiments demonstrate how simple changes to your daily routine and lighting at home can help you and your family to see the silver lining, even when the sun seems light years away.

Wherever you go, no matter what the weather, always bring your own sunshine.

Anthony J. D'Angelo American entrepreneur and author

What you can do!

Embrace the 'blue' hour

Your happy hormones are likely to be at their lowest ebb in the hours before dawn. Your core temperature and blood pressure are also down, and sleep pressure will be draining away.

If you've had a broken night, this can be when you lie awake dreading the alarm clock, knowing that the stresses of the day are about to burst into view. And yet, the 'blue hour' can not only help you to get a better night's sleep the next day, but it can also help to chase away that early morning mist.

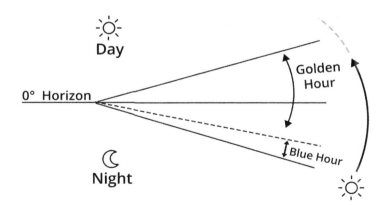

The Blue Hour

That's because just before dawn, the sun is below the horizon. As a result, the light you see is not coming directly to you but is bouncing down from the ozone layer. As a result, it is full of the sky blue wavelengths that give a unique boost to your body clock, mood-regulating and alerting pathways.

You will reinforce this rise-and-shine signal if you can physically get up and move around, even if you cannot get outside. That's because your body clock primes every system in your body before your normal wake-up time to prepare for the day. So if you can just stand up and draw the curtains, you will be helping your brain to greet the day.

Power up

You will get the maximum lift from light in the morning. But bright light at any time of the day can break through the gloom to power up your mood-boosting system. That's because it not only lets your body clock know it's time to be up and about but also plugs in your alerting and a cascade of reward-seeking systems, including dopamine, serotonin and endorphins.

The amount of light you need is not an exact science. That's because everyones' eyes are different - for example, people with blue eyes and lighter colouring need much less than those who are naturally darker-skinned. In addition, people experiencing depression tend to have lower levels of these hormones to start with, so they need a bit more help.

But most scientists agree that 30 minutes outside in natural sunlight, ideally at the same time every morning is an excellent place to start. SAD lamps are designed to deliver this minimum dose. But sunlight provides some other unique benefits that most lamps don't deliver. That's because sunlight offers a range of wavelengths beyond the visible spectrum that your eyes can 'see'. The wavelengths that matter for mood are the longer wavelengths known as UVA and UVB. Your eyes and skin use these wavelengths to transform minerals in your diet to build Vitamin D. Vitamin D, as we will see in the next chapter, is not only vital for brain performance, but it also helps to stabilise hormone levels so that you enjoy a sustained peaceful, optimistic mood. Scientists draw clear links between low Vitamin D levels, seasonal depression and a whole range of other mental health issues that more and more young people wrestle with today. [44]

Encouraging students to get outside for regular breaks has been shown to help them feel happier and more alert in other ways, too: they breathe more deeply, which in turn boosts oxygen levels in the brain; you improve balance, hand-eye coordination and blink rate, which in turn enhances hydration and helps to ease eye strain and computer vision syndrome [45].

Take control

People who feel they have more control over their environment tend to be healthier, happier, and more resistant to disease. Equally, making active decisions about the quality of light in your space can boost your mood. In particular, the ability to create a sense of 'prospect' and open vistas or refuge where you can feel secluded and secure can have a powerful impact on mood. A loss of pleasure, feeling overwhelmed, and reduced ability to connect with the outside world are tell-tale signs of depression. Equally, we are alert to every delightful detail when we are happy. We are alive to emotions and enjoy opening up to share with others.

Light can help give us a sense of control, hope and value when feeling depressed. Studies show that employees tend to be happier, more productive, and take less sick leave when they feel valued. [46]

Research into employee engagement suggests lighting is often seen as a proxy or substitute for a broader attitude to employee relations. For example, one study about how to attract the best employees found that up to 40% of candidates admit to turning down a job when the office and interview space look gloomy.

By contrast, giving teams a sense of control [47]-and even simply asking the employee what they would like, contributes to a strong employer brand which translates directly to better financial results[48].

The same applies to your relationships at home: showing those around you that you care for their health and happiness can spark a positive cycle of kindness and consideration,

Set the tone

Experiment with different light sources - overhead lights, spotlights, task lights and low-level side lamps- and more playful options such as colourful LED strips and disco lights so you can shift the mood with the touch of a button or screen.

Consider the light fittings where you spend the most time to ensure that all the shades are clean and that all the lightbulbs and controls work as they should.

Consider flooding the space where you spend time in the morning with bright cool light to create the impression of a fresh spring day. Bouncing lights from the ceiling or a brightly-coloured feature wall can deliver a sky dome feeling and cut down on glare and harsh shadows. Complement those visual cues with the smell of coffee and a favourite soundtrack.

Small touches like a welcoming lamp in the hallway or an upgrade to the task light for a child's desk can send a powerful signal to your friends and family, guests and colleagues that you value and care for them.

Highlight happy times

Another approach that has been shown to boost mental health is to use light to trigger a happy memory and create a sense of wonder. This simple reminder can trigger the initial physiological response, including 'happy' hormones. Not only does this change your chemistry at that moment, but it can also begin to alter the balance of hormones to build a virtuous positive cycle.

A spotlight directed onto a photograph, a souvenir, a plant or an object that reminds you of that time can be an effortless way to boost your mood. The light source itself can perform a similar role: a favourite lantern or fairy lights can evoke strong memories of friendships and situations from the past. Using light to create miniature 'scenes' can also help you imagine an ideal future that your mind's eye can bring into being.

Although nothing beats the 'real thing', a simple reminder of the natural world's beauty and wonder can help calm the mind.

What about...

Answers to some of the questions that people ask me most often.

SAD lamps?

When you can't get outside- and for dark winter days when the light levels do not reach the threshold your mood system needs, a well-designed 'SAD' lamp can provide some light relief.

Generally, SAD lamps are designed to emit light with a brightness level of at least 10,000 lux, equivalent to the intensity of natural sunlight on a clear day. Lux is an international standard that describes light intensity perceived by the human eye. Research suggests that 10,000 lux is the minimum threshold for therapeutic light exposure. You can achieve this light level with a typical SAD lamp around 30-60cm from the face.

The optimal duration of light therapy also varies. However, it typically ranges from 30 minutes to 2 hours per day, depending on the intensity of the lamp and the severity of the symptoms. Check the manufacturer's instructions and consult a healthcare professional before using a SAD lamp. These techniques are not a replacement for professional advice, and overexposure to bright light can cause eye strain, headaches, and other side effects.

Dawn simulator lamps?

These lamps provide an alternative to the sudden wake-up signal delivered by an alarm clock or phone by gradually increasing light levels and a gentle shift from soft and warm to bright and cool light. Research suggests that dawn simulator lamps can offer some relief for people experiencing symptoms of Seasonal Affective Disorder.[49]

Sunlight - isn't it dangerous!

The ozone layer depletion that filters out harmful wavelengths means that UV levels are rising to dangerous levels in many countries, including the UK. So the Apple Weather App now includes UV levels to indicate this measurement's importance.

But you can get the benefits of sunlight - including reducing the risk of allergies including eczema [50] manage your exposure carefully and use simple protective measures - going outside early in the day or late in the afternoon, using sunscreen, sunglasses and protective clothing. Depending on your skin, 30 minutes in natural daylight before 9 am, under dappled shade if the sun is already too warm for comfort, is likely to give you a natural high without causing harm.

Most experts agree that babies under six months should be kept in the shade rather than full sunlight. Their skin is so delicate that sunscreen can irritate their skin and even trigger allergic reactions.

Does sunscreen help?

While sunscreen can help protect your skin from harmful UV radiation, it can also block some wavelengths of light needed to boost your mood. Specifically, sunscreen that contains UV filters can block UVB radiation, which is responsible for the production of vitamin D in the skin.

Some newer types of sunscreens have been designed to allow some beneficial wavelengths of light, while protecting against harmful UV radiation. These sunscreens, known as "broad-spectrum", contain ingredients that help filter out UVA and UVB radiation while still allowing some visible light to get through to your skin.

However, recent research suggests that some sunscreens may contain ingredients that carry long term health risks and can contaminate waterways, so it's worth looking at the label: oxybenzone and retinyl palmitate are two of the chemicals that ingredients can cause skin irritation, allergic reactions, and hormone disruption.

Minerals that physically block UV wavelengths, such as zinc oxide and titanium dioxide,are generally considered safe for children and adults alike. [51]

Consider spending brief periods of time outdoors without sunscreen during non-peak hours and following safe sun practices to minimise the risk of skin damage. However, it is vital to balance the potential benefits of sunlight exposure with the need to protect your skin from damage.

What about sunscreen for small children?

It is important to protect their delicate skin so choose a broad-spectrum sunscreen with an SPF of at least 30 and apply it generously to all exposed skin, including the face, ears, and neck. Apply the lotion at least 15-30 minutes before going outside and to reapply every two hours - more often if the child has been swimming or running around.

In addition to using sunscreen, use protective clothing, such as hats, long-sleeved shirts, and pants, and seek shade during peak sunlight hours.

Does sun-protective clothing work?

Protective clothing with a UPF (Ultraviolet Protection Factor) rating is designed to protect the skin from the harmful effects of UV radiation.

The UPF rating measures how much UV radiation can penetrate the fabric and reach the skin. A higher UPF rating means more UV radiation is blocked by the material, providing better protection for the skin. For example, a shirt with a UPF rating of 50 will allow 98% (or 1/50th of the UV radiation) to get through the fabric and reach the skin, providing high protection.

Protective clothing with a UPF rating is made from tightly woven fabrics with a higher thread count or special additives that block UV radiation. The material's colour can also affect its UPF rating, with darker colours generally providing more protection than lighter colours.

It is important to note that protective clothing with a UPF rating should still be used with other sun protection measures, such as wearing a hat and sunglasses, seeking shade, and using sunscreen on exposed skin. It is also essential to follow the care instructions for the clothing, as washing and wearing can affect the UPF rating over time.

Sunglasses - will they block the effects?

Wearing sunglasses will not reduce the benefits of sunshine on mood, because most models will let sunlight into your eyes as it reflects on your skin. In fact, ski goggles that fit closely to the face are the only kind of glasses that effectively block all UV exposure.

Wearing sunglasses can even have some indirect benefits for your mood because you're not squinting or straining your eyes, which can lead to headaches and discomfort. By reducing these symptoms, sunglasses may help people feel more comfortable and relaxed outdoors, contributing to a more positive mood overall. [52]

Sunglasses - what should I buy?

When shopping for sunglasses, choosing lenses that provide adequate protection against harmful UV rays is essential. Look for sunglasses with 100% UV protection or a UV 400 rating, which means they block all UV rays 400 nanometers or less in wavelength.

Additionally, consider the lens colour and darkness. Specialists often recommend grey lenses because they make colours look the most natural. Brown or amber lenses can enhance contrast and depth perception, which might be a consideration if you're playing a sport such as golf. The darkness of the lenses can also affect how well you can see in different lighting conditions. Reactive lenses can offer the best of both worlds, but check the response times - a slow reaction can be dangerous when driving from bright sunshine into a dark a tunnel.

When buying sunglasses, it's also a good idea to check the label or packaging to ensure they comply with your country's safety standards. For example, in the US, sunglasses must meet the standards set by the American National Standards Institute (ANSI) or the Food and Drug Administration (FDA) to ensure adequate protection.

Consider the design, too: Choose a 'wrap-around' design with big, wide lenses, ideally with lenses mounted on the arms to cut down on stray light and reflections from your skin. These features are especially critical if you spend time on the water in snowy or desert conditions because sunlight bounces from the ground and the sky. Add a hat with a broad brim to cut down glare and reflections from the sky.

Sitting by the window - as good as going outside?

Sitting by a window can provide some of the benefits of sunshine, but it depends on the type of window and how clean it is!

Most windows, including car windshields, are designed to block UVB rays but still let UVA through which can cause skin damage that increases the risk of cancer.

Sitting by a window can be a great way to bathe in the mood-boosting connection with nature and the turbo-charging effect of bright light. But unless you are actually getting direct sunlight, this filtered version doesn't deliver the full rainbow of mood-brightening benefits.

"Happiness can be found in even the darkest times, if only one remembers to turn on the light."

J.K Rowling

Author

'Killer arguments'

All the young people I know are acutely aware of just how important it is to take care of their mental health. A distressing number have experienced first-hand the devastating effects of self-harm, bullying and even suicide. Here are some facts and tips they might find useful. Just don't say 'I told you so!'

Why does mood matter?

People who feel happier overall...

O Are healthier and take less time off school: Students with mental health issues took an average of 13.5% more days off sick from school and were at a 31% higher risk of severe COVID-19 infection.[53]

O Find it easier to solve problems and be constructive: An active positive (happy) mood can boost your ability to come up with alternative solutions by up to 27% whereas a neutral or negative mood makes you more likely to see the downsides of an argument. Managing anxiety can boost achievement by up to a full letter grade.[54]

O Have more active and positive social networks: people with depression are ten times more likely than average to report feeling lonely [55]. Equally, thinking about friends can make the reward and motivation parts of your brain light up [56].

What's light got to do with it?

O Your eyes have a hotline to the parts of your brain that regulate 'happy' hormones including serotonin and dopamine. Bright light gives those systems a boost[57].

O Daylight gives the best results because it includes wavelengths that help your brain to make Vitamin D, which also helps you to feel relaxed and happy. Most artificial lights just don't have those extra wavelengths[58].

O Your brain looks at the quality of your environment and decides whether you are in a place where you are valued and safe. The light - natural daylight and artificial light - has a big part to play [59].

So what can you do?

O Get outside - 30 minutes in sunlight every day is the minimum. But it doesn't have to be in a single session. Morning is best - it will help you to sleep too. But anytime is fine.

O Boost through the winter: You might need a special high-powered lamp known as a SAD lamp to help you get through the darkest months of the winter. Make sure that's set up in a place where you can use it every day - next to your desk for example.

O Take a look at your room to see if you can make it feel like a place you want to be. Are the windows clean and do the curtains work? Do all the lights work and can you change them to give you a feeling of welcome and comfort? [60]

Conclusion

As parents and godparents, aunts and uncles, friends and neighbours, we all want these precious young people to feel happy and balanced. We see first-hand the long shadow that poor mental health casts across our precious next generation. We lie awake wondering when they will emerge from the dark tunnel of depression to enjoy the bright future they so richly deserve. We invest everything we have to give them the best start.

And yet we often ignore the ABC of mental health: the life-affirming power of light. Bright light is better than an antidepressant to cut through the gloom and help them to feel alive. An atmosphere of care, connection with nature and reminders of happy times will allow them to build a sense of perspective. Simple controls will encourage them to find their own sparkle and confidence in an uncertain world.

"You are my sunshine, my only sunshine, you make me happy when skies are grey!"

Jimmie Davis and Charles Mitchell

Singer-Songwriters

Checklist to boost your mood

1. Do you get outside every morning for at least 30 minutes?

2. If you suffer from low mood in the winter, have you considered investing in a SAD lamp? (And do you use it every morning?)

3. Is the lighting comfortable and uplifting?

    1. All the lights working and clean?

    2. Views of nature, though a window, to plants or other natural materials?

    3. Accent lights on reminders of happy times?

    4. Controls to suit mood and adjust ambience?

Further reading

I've put links and academic papers online so it's easier for you to track them down. I can check and update them more easily too. Please use this QR code

3/ Be Brilliant

"If knowledge is power, then learning is a superpower."

Jim Kwik

American brain coach, podcaster, writer, and entrepreneur

Introduction

Helping a child discover the world may be one of the most rewarding and exciting jobs most of us will ever do. We all have memories of an inspiring teacher and 'lightbulb moments' that sparked a lifelong passion for a subject, sport, craft, or language and hope to offer the same gift to the young people around us too.

Being part of a child's learning journey is also a great responsibility: you know just how much a solid education can help them to become the resilient, confident and successful adults you know they can be. You may be worried that they struggle to focus at school: around one in ten students experience learning difficulty, from sensory processing to concentration, managing emotions and disruptive behaviour.

As a parent, you may be keen to take care of your own brain too so you can keep up with your children- for as long as possible, at least! You know that your memory is a muscle like any other, so you need to 'use it or lose it'. Your interest in learning may go beyond your role as a formal or informal teacher. You may also want to be able to speak confidently and remember names and details in a meeting or a family occasion without relying on notes or worrying that your brain will 'go blank'.

Luckily, memory is a muscle that you can train at any age. Light can help in three key ways. The first is the motivation to learn in the first place. That means an environment where we feel valued and reminded that we can achieve our highest goals with persistence and creativity. The second is a space where we are physically comfortable and can focus on the task. The third is a daily routine, including optimising timing for learning, rest and diet and sunlight that will keep their growing brains healthy and able to 'fire and wire' with ease.

A growing number of schools worldwide are harnessing the power of light to support learning: research shows that investing in the quality of the environment can boost student attainment by up to 17%[61]. A better working environment is good for teachers, too: one study suggested that a space where staff felt valued and able to do their job was as important to them as pay[62].

In this chapter, you will learn about learning and memory and how to use light to support them to fulfil their potential and become their brilliant selves.

"Education is power. It is just like a light in complete darkness."

Ziauddin Yousafzai

Pakistani education activist, father of Nobel laureate Malala Yousafzai

How do you learn?

Your brain is constantly sorting through an avalanche of data all the time. First, you need to decide that the information will be significant enough to commit attention and resources to store that knowledge in the first place. So the first vital step in learning is focused attention. While you read this sentence, your brain is firing across temporary neural connections, similar to writing with chalk on a blackboard. Most people can hold a handful, perhaps five to seven, concepts, actions or data points in this short-term working memory for around 15-30 seconds. That natural grouping is why most passwords and PIN numbers contain up to seven digits.

We are more likely to remember situations that trigger strong feelings because that learning is likely to be useful- whether to make sure we avoid or seek out a similar situation in the future. That emotional anchoring is why we find words, sounds or images that evoke physical sensations so much more memorable than neutral ones.

The next step of this process is known as association. Like a jigsaw puzzle, you will find it easier to store new information if it is connected with an established framework of understanding. For example, once you have a basic knowledge of a city, you will find it easier to remember a new route down a back street.

The more learning modes - seeing, speaking or writing, for example - that you can use to build those bridges between existing and new knowledge, the more neural connections you will make and the easier it will be to remember the information. The Memory Palace technique is one application of this principle. You associate a fact or element of knowledge with a familiar place to create a sequence or story. Once you retrieve the first anchor point in the series, you can follow the thread around the room. The more sensory dimensions you can load onto each anchor - the quality of light, for example - the more information you can retain.

Your brain uploads information into long-term storage during 'REM' or rapid-eye-movement sleep. Scans of sleeping brains show the hippocampus communicating with the neocortex, the deeply-folded outer layers of the brain, reactivating and rehearsing the connections involved in the original acquisition. This rehearsing and uploading reinforces neural pathways so that, over time, these patterns of explicit understanding become tacit knowledge or habits.

The process of acquisition, association and consolidation demands flexibility and resilience. Vitamin D is vital to this process: it acts like a 'glue' to stabilise neural connections and boost levels of the motivation and reward hormones reviewed in the previous chapter.

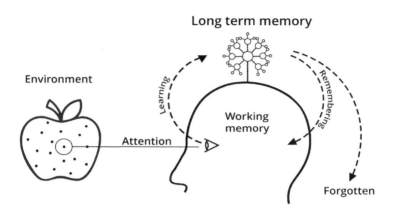

Memory cycle

"Neither comprehension nor learning can take place in an atmosphere of anxiety."

Rose Kennedy

American philanthropist and socialite

What you can do!

Boost motivation

We remember the things we value. For example, a child learning to walk is determined and persistent. They keep getting up until they are soon skipping and running around.

We know that some pressure to learn knowledge or skill is valuable because it helps us to overcome inertia. However, beyond a certain level, healthy stress slides into anxiety and avoidance.

When your child studies in an environment where they feel valued and reassured, they are more likely to keep going even when the going gets tough. For example, making sure that their workspace is set up for their comfort and making sure that they have all the tools they need- including your attention when they need it - will help to boost their confidence.

A spotlight or a string of fairy lights that draws your attention to an image, an object, or a phrase that reminds you of your goals and people you admire can also help to keep you on track. High-performance athletes use similar techniques and often keep photographs and mementoes in their lockers for a quick motivational boost before a workout or a match.

Focus

Bright light has a hotline to the alerting systems in the hypothalamus. You can see this powerful automatic response for yourself: the pupil automatically contracts within milliseconds of a burst of bright light. Bright light triggers a cocktail of other physiological reactions too: your heart beats faster, the sweat glands on your skin open, reaction times accelerate, and your working memory ramps up.

We naturally associate bright cool light, particularly from above, with being wide awake, active and visible to others. That tends to lead to behaviour that is more goal-oriented and pro-social. Creating those conditions in the learning space will encourage a sense of motivation towards an external goal - an exam result, for example. Work with young children has found that bright cool light can even improve reading fluency and speed.[63]

As we have seen in the chapter on sleep, not only does bright light boost alertness, it critically helps us to stay focused in the face of distractions. That ability to sustain concentration is vital to learning and memory formation. Serotonin is another hormone that helps with memory formation and mood, as seen in the previous chapter. Here again, bright light, particularly sunlight, has been shown to boost serotonin levels in the brain.

Everyone is different, but around 500 lux at the eye is the minimum you need to sustain concentration - download one of the free online apps (link in the references and the QR code) and measure the levels from your desk in the morning and afternoon.

Timing

Your body clock is optimised to perform different tasks throughout the day—for example, the sex hormones testosterone and progesterone peak in the first few hours after waking. Their optimal timing depends on your personal chronotype, as discussed in the previous chapter. Teen body clocks are running around two hours later than an adults', so their optimal times will be different.

But the basic pattern or sequence is the same. The first hours after waking are optimal for visualising, strategic thinking and journaling, 'priming' the body and brain for challenges of the day to come. Your mental focus tends to peak around five hours after waking, making this the best time for tasks that involve sustained concentration and precision. This 'sharp' brain tends to shift in to a more social and collaborative mode by around noon and into the early afternoon. This is the ideal time for for planning, collaboration and coordination with others.

Muscle tone, flexibility and coordination will come together in the late afternoon, with cardiovascular strength and efficiency peaking around sunset. For our ancestors, this was when animals were on the move and the perfect time to hunt. So it's perhaps not surprising that most sporting records are broken in the late afternoon [64].

Encourage them to track the times of the day when they are most focused and alert and make the most of these for intense study. This will encourage them to take control of their own study routine, which will be a vital skill for them in their personal and professional lives in future.

The protege effect

 It can be hard to convince a student to switch off the screen in good time - they have so much homework to do and need time to catch up with their friends too. But if

you can encourage them to spend the two hours before sleep rehearsing - or better yet - teaching - a topic that they understand to someone else, they can boost their results by up to a full grade point. This mechanism, known as the 'protege' or 'learning by teaching' effect not only increases recall. engagement and confidence in the subject, it is also linked to another strategy, known as the testing effect, where students are able to identify gaps in knowledge before study and focus their revision on the areas that are most beneficial. One project showed that recall was almost doubled in a 'test-study' sequence compared to the standard 'study-test'[65].

Many students get a 'second wind' in the early evening, especially if they feel anxious about an exam or deadline. They can then be tempted to keep going. That drive is not helped by the impression that all their friends are wide awake and working. They may feel that switching off means they are dull or lazy, which adds to the pressure to stay awake. However, research consistently shows that students get better results - up to 24.4% in one study - if they switch off rather than burn the midnight oil[66].

Power down screens and sources of bright 'cool' light and switch to post-it notes, a white board or coloured pens and paper. Encourage them to use diagrams or physical models and craft materials to generate a visual expression of an idea or a principle. The ability to communicate clearly will not only help them to remember the information, it will be a valuable skill in their professional and personal lives.

Spaced repetition

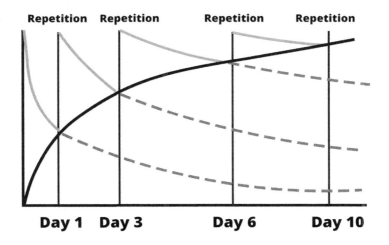

Remembering through repetition

These strategies are linked to another tried and tested learning principle, spaced repetition' [67]. Students who switch between related topics and combine modalities - writing, mind-mapping alone or with others, reading and listening to a podcast, for example - you find it easier to remember and make connections with existing knowledge. This bridging increases the strength of the memory.

You can switch between lighting ambiences or even create shelves with coloured LEDs to help them to anchor and associate different kinds of information.

See the wood for the trees

Computers and phones are incredible storage systems and becoming more sophisticated every day. For example, most of us only know a handful of phone numbers and passwords and delegate the rest to the cloud. In principle, this frees up processing power to focus on higher-level functions. But the problem with this undifferentiated capture is that we never have to decide which data is valuable or what is merely background noise.

As a result, we have lost the art of choosing and combining information to create new knowledge, like a computer desktop littered with unmarked folders. That's a problem because working memory uses the 'mind's eye', where order and clarity are essential[68].

So visual clutter drains bandwidth and reduces working memory capacity. Recent research shows that visual clutter can even reduce our ability to read racial expressions and increase irritation and aggression[69].

It may be helpful to think of the principle like a kitchen: when the worktops are cluttered, it is harder to work efficiently. Equally, a workspace that is too sterile can limit creative lateral associations - just as having different ingredients in a space can trigger fresh ideas for a new recipe.

Most of us are happiest with a balance of predictability and surprise. But as a general rule, the most comfortable patterns of light and shade for sustained concentration are as close to nature as possible without extreme reflections or distracting movement.

Consider the view from where you sit to work and arrange the light sources to create a tidy and well-organised vista with clear space around a bright point of focus - the book, the screen or the keyboard, for example.

Light can help you to create a clear hierarchy of information - simply adding a task light to create a patch of bright light on your notes - or using simple clip-on lights on your revision schedule and task list will help you to keep focused and avoid distractions.

Memory palace

You can harness the power of your minds' eye to turbo-charge anchoring in the Memory Palace technique. Consider using specific colours or types of light (candle light, a bedside lamp or a chandelier), or even associate different natural lighting conditions (bright sunshine, a glowing sunset of the glowering clouds before a storm) with different points, emotions or steps in a process that you want to remember[70].

Reset

A related principle is known as Attention Restoration Theory. After a period of focused work, your brain can feel overloaded and tired. Lighting reminds us of our connection with nature. For example, bouncing light from natural textures has been found to restore attention and mental focus. Studies show that we often find textures and patterns that create a varied but balanced range of tones and scales more attractive, interesting, arousing, and fascinating.

Scans even show increased activity in the brain's pleasure centres[71].

Going for a walk around the block or simply standing on the doorstep has another benefit for memory, particularly semantic knowledge - names and facts, for example. When you rehearse the argument or activity in different environments, you will likely find it easier to remember them later.

You may have seen this principle in action if you have seen a familiar face out of context and struggled to remember the person's name. So a change of scene or context is a great way to check and boost your memory. You don't have to go outside to create this context shift. You can also achieve this by switching the lights or changing to a different desk or physical position.

Diet

As well as its vital role in mood regulation, Vitamin D works like a flexible glue to help neural connections form and remain stable and its essential role in mood regulation. Recent research indicates that low Vitamin D levels may be linked to memory loss in people with dementia[72]. Sunshine and a healthy diet boosted with supplements during the winter months and for those who struggle to maintain healthy levels naturally will help to keep your muscle memory in good shape.

What about...

Coloured filters for students with Autism Spectrum Disorder?

Children with ASD often experience visual stress, including the experience of objects and letters appearing to 'jump around' or become blurry. Some of these effects were grouped into a syndrome known as scotopic sensitivity syndrome and later called Meares-Irlen, or simply Irlen. There have been a number of small-scale studies that suggest that overlays or tinted glasses can make a significant difference to reading speed, emotion recognition and communication, while reducing visual stress and other related symptoms such as headaches [73]. However, other systematic reviews suggest there is not currently enough robust scientific evidence to confirm that this approach will definitely help.

Outside views for students with Autism Spectrum Disorder?

Students who struggle to concentrate can find that windows with outside views are distracting. However they also need the dynamic qualities of daylight and the mood-enhancing influence of this vital connection with nature and the outside world. One practical solution can be to add a 'frosted' or semi-transparent panel to the lower portion of the window to reduce the distraction while still allowing a view of the sky.

Sensory rooms?

For students who are experiencing emotional or sensory overload, a self-contained space where they can control the sensory environment can provide a vital circuit-breaker. Light has a valuable part to play . This may include simply increasing or dimming the light levels or encouraging them to play with coloured lights to create a calming or playful ambience.

The quality and integration of light fittings and controls are key in this setting: there can be an increased risk of flicker and hum if they're not working together correctly. This can be a particular problem for these young people who are extremely sensitive to high-frequency movement and sound. Low-tech solutions such as torches, filters and safe reflective materials can be as effective.

Students who experience extreme fatigue and other symptoms linked to their menstrual cycle?

The hormone cycle affects every young person differently, but changes to energy levels, migraine headaches and visual stress are a common concern.

Some migraines have been linked to low levels of melatonin, so getting outside in the morning and making sure they switch off in good time will help to set their body clock, increasing the levels of melatonin released at night. Sunlight will also help them to metabolise Vitamin D, which has been shown to have an anti-inflammatory effect - another symptom of the menstrual cycle [74].

Lighting can help to create calm and comforting space to rest- but encourage them to get outside to boost their mood and vitamin D levels too.

'Killer arguments'

Some young people find learning a breeze. Others can find school a dismal struggle and react strongly to any suggestions, however well-meaning you may be. Here are some facts that just might encourage the students in your life to discover the joy of learning for themselves.

Why does learning matter?

O Better grades lead to better pay. Four years after graduation students with the lowest grades at law school who worked in private legal practice earned around 60% of the pay of students with the highest grades[75].

O Education leads to better health. By the age of 30 those with the highest levels of education are expected to live four years longer than those with the lowest levels of education. Graduating from college gives you a one-third lower risk of heart disease[76].

O College graduates have more extensive systems of social support and a larger number of close friends too. They are likely to report feeling lonely and isolated less often in later life, perhaps due to better health and higher socio-economic status[77].

What's light got to do with it?

o Timing. A simple routine including bright light in the morning and warm light to rehearse the lessons from the day and a dark room to sleep will set your body clock and help you get the deep sleep you need to learn. That light-warm-dark cycle will allow you to time your study for optimal performance: you can can even boost your grades by the equivalent of six IQ points by taking exams when you are most alert: afternoon for most adolescents because of the natural delay in your body clock[78].

o Working Memory: Lighting that creates complex shadows or glare reduces working memory because they compete for attention and contribute to eye strain. You are likely to make more mistakes and react more slowly in a space that is cluttered and uncomfortable,

o Alerting effects. Bright 'cool' light can halve your reaction times, while daylight is better than a shot of coffee to beat the post-lunch dip, even if you are sleep deprived.

So what can you do?

Set your body clock up for success.

Set up your workspace for comfort and control

Get enough bright light during the day - daylight when you can but bright cool LED lights will help a lot.

Conclusion

You were born to learn, as anyone who has spent time with a small child will know.

Lighting can help you to create the optimal conditions for learning, boosting focus, attention and motivation too. Experiment to find the perfect balance of focus and calm so that you can support these curious young minds to discover the joy of learning and become their brilliant best. Guide them to choose the right light for the task: bright and cool for a rapid-fire response, warm and relaxed for reflection and lateral thinking. Use the emotional dimension of light to build a vivid memory palace that will stand out in their mind's eye. Time their study for peak performance, make sure they get plenty of sleep and serve up a nutritious diet that helps their growing brain to build secure connections for a bright future.

"If you think education is expensive, try estimating the cost of ignorance."

Howard Gardner

American cognitive psychologist

Checklist for Learning

1. Do you know your child's ideal time for learning?

2. Do you schedule a break with them to go outside at least three times per day? (morning, lunchtime and afternoon)

3. Does the area where they study ...

   O have access to a window with a view?

   O have enough bright light to keep them alert?

   O Give easy ways to cut out glare from screens, windows and other reflective surfaces?

   O give a tidy view from their chair?

   O give the option to shift to softer warm light with access to alternative learning (paper, pens, craft materials, white board etc.) to revise before bed?

Further reading

Please use this QR code for links to books and papers.

4/ Light and the Brain

"The eyes are the gateway to the soul."

Herman Melville

American novelist and poet

Introduction

You don't need to know any of this to make the most of the suggestions in the rest of the book. But, if like me, you always want to know the 'why' behind a suggestion, this chapter will give you a quick 'refresher' on how the eye and brain grow and how they work.

Seeing a child's eyes light up makes your heart sing. You feel a warm glow of tenderness as their eyelids softly close in sleep and know just how precious their sensitive young eyes really are. You may worry when they want to hide away from bright light and see them suffer from crippling headaches that can leave them in a dark room for days. You know the hours they spend hunched over their screens make them tired and irritable. But you don't want to be nagging them all the time. So just like the other chapters, I've some 'killer arguments' so they can make better choices for themselves when they're ready.

"A happy baby has shining eyes. It walks open-hearted into the world and spreads magic."

Sigrid Leo

Author

How does it work?

Eyes

Your eyes start to form in the first week of life[79]. By seven weeks, you already have the light-sensing cells you need to send signals from your eyes to your central nervous system. Your body clock will be marking time after just three months. Your eyes will continue to grow after birth right the way to adolescence, shaped like a plant, by food and water and by the amount of light you give them.

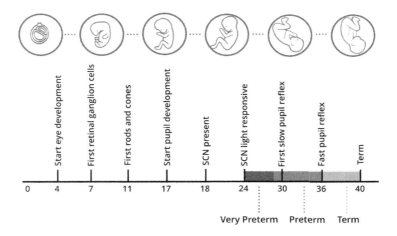

From Hazelhoff, Dudink et al (2021)

Around half of the factors determining whether your children will enjoy 20:20 vision is down to their genes. But you might be surprised to know just how much difference the environment, especially the light, can make.

For example, your eyes grow by around 65% from birth to adolescence[80]. Like a plant, when the eye does not get enough light, it becomes elongated and weak, leading to myopia. Spending just two hours outside per day can reduce the risk of myopia by 40%[81] [82].

The same goes for their ability to handle bright light, also known as photosensitivity or photophobia. You can create stimulating and comfortable lighting conditions in their early years that will shape their visual health for the rest of their lives.

The problem is that babies and children don't know what is 'normal' and can't explain what they see - or don't see. The world may be a blurry and frightening place to them, so it's not surprising that they become disruptive or withdrawn. Students diagnosed with Attention Deficit Disorder are three times more likely than average children to have a problem with vision too[83].

The window to the soul?

You can certainly tell a lot about someone by looking into their eyes. The Greeks believed that crystalline spirits played just behind the coloured iris. As late as the 17th Century, the French philosopher Descartes

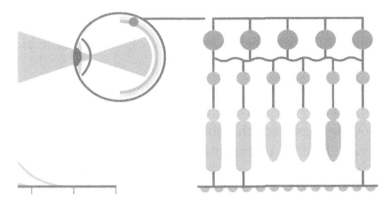

Retina: rods and cones (bottom layer), ipRGCs (top layer)

believed that you sent eye beams, like ambassadors out in to the world to bring back information. Iridologists believe that you can diagnose conditions by analysing the textures and colours of the iris - the coloured disc at the front of the eye. You may always have brown or blue eyes, you may be surprised to see how much the colours and patterns can change over time.

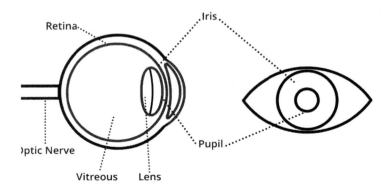

Structure of the eye

The whites of your eyes also reflect the state of your health overall: when you are dehydrated or running low on essential fats, vitamins and minerals, for example[84].

You may be surprised to know that you can even tell how well your brain is doing if you look through the pupil or window at the front of the eye to inspect the light-sensitive tissue at the back of the eye called the retina[85]. That's because the cells in your retina are closely related to the cells in your brain. In the early days of space flight, doctors didn't have access to the instant digital scans they do today. So they looked into the astronauts' eyes to track how their brains were coping with life in zero gravity.

Pupil

The muscles that open and close the pupil are directly linked to your central nervous system. It is one of the most immediate and reliable signs that you are conscious. For example, you may notice that paramedics shine a flashlight into the eye of a casualty. When you are relaxed, the pupil tends to open wider.

Your pupil works like a dynamic window. It's constantly changing size to let in more or less light. So your pupil will open wide when the light levels are low to capture as much detail as you can. But, equally, it will close down when it's bright outside to protect the retina.

Your eyes evolved to operate in the natural world where the brightest zones are around twice the level of the darkest areas. So your eyes are most comfortable when the lighting in your home or office has a similar contrast range.

But students often stare at a bright computer screen in a dark room - or strain their eyes to make out the text on a dim screen or whiteboard in a classroom where the glare from a window or overhead light creates extreme contrast. After a while, you may notice they rub their eyes or complain of a headache. That may be because the pupil or 'window' cannot decide whether it should be wide open to capture enough light to see the darker areas or close down to avoid damaging the retina.

Intense light in the evening, particularly the high-energy blue wavelengths from computer screens, may be especially harmful to young eyes, which are much more transparent and flexible than older ones[86].

Like any other muscle in their growing body, the muscles that drive the pupil response need a healthy diet to stay flexible and healthy. So even if they are fair-skinned or naturally sensitive to light, you can give the 'window of the soul' a helping hand.

Retina

The retina is a delicate multilayered membrane, an extension of the brain that starts to form in the first few weeks of life. The bottom layer is packed with two types of cells: rods and cones.

Most of the light-sensing cells in your eyes are known as rods. These grow around the edge of the retina and work best in low light conditions.

Some believe that they are a legacy of a time in our evolutionary history when we had to hide from dinosaurs during the day and could only come out at night.

The second type are called cones because of their shape and evolved to give us colour vision. Cones are packed into a dip in the centre of the eye known as the fovea or macular. Your eyes naturally move around, so this colour-sensitive section is directly behind the pupil. There are three types of cones, each sensitive to different wavelengths or colours of light. Your brain blends those signals to create your experience of colour.

Colour vision

About 1 in 12 boys and 1 in 200 girls experience some form of colour blindness, usually because the cones are working in an unusual way. That means that there are likely to be two boys in every class who see colours differently.

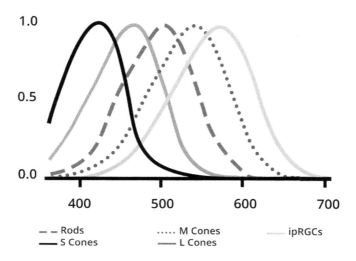

Rods, cones and ipRGCs are sensitive to different wavelengths or colours

As a result, it may be hard for some people to tell the difference between specific colours[87].

At the other end of the spectrum, a very small number of women have an extra cone that is sensitive to the green part of the spectrum[88].

When babies are born, the connections that create colour vision are still under construction, so most can only see contrast - the difference between dark and light tones. However, this skill develops over time until the colour perception pathway is fully up and running by around three months of age.

But the ability to 'see' the colours is only part of the equation. As we will see in the next section about the brain, only around 70% of your experience of sight is generated from new data from your eyes[89]. Your brain makes up the rest based on knowledge gained during the first days and weeks of life when you trained your eyes to see.

There is no known 'cure' for colour blindness, but you can use lighting to manage the condition. The first point is to ensure that your space's lighting offers good colour rendering - discussed in more detail in the next chapter on how to buy lights.

Special lenses or glasses can also enhance the appearance of colours. Software or apps offer another solution because they allow users to adjust colours on a computer or phone screen to make them more distinguishable.

You can also experiment with a variety of lighting hues to add variety and interest for people who see colours differently.

Seeing depth

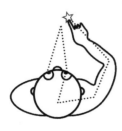 Your left and right eyes are positioned on either side of your nose - around 6cm apart. That means your left and right eyes get slightly different views of the world. You can see that if you close one eye and then the other. Your brain calculates the difference between these two images to

create your experience of objects in depth. Your brain also uses this difference to judge how fast something is moving.

This 'adding up' process, known as binocular vision, makes little difference when objects are far away - as you will see if you look at an object on the other side of the room. But this ability to see the three-dimensional shapes is vital to survival when things - or other people - get closer. This is because your depth perception really comes into its own at around two meters - or the length of your two arms outstretched.

You need to train the muscles around your eyes to point together correctly. This gives your body the information it needs to develop hand-eye coordination - which is essential for sports where you need to be able to hit or catch a fast-moving object or intercept a player on the opposing team. The problem comes when babies spend a lot of time looking at flat screens. They simply don't get enough practice interpreting signals from a three-dimensional world.

Many babies are born with crossed eyes, a condition known as infantile strabismus. That is often because those eye muscles still need to develop fully, and the condition usually corrects itself over time. Some

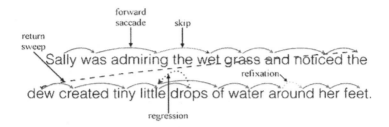

How your eye moves when reading text. The jumps are known as 'saccades'.

therapists use torches and other light sources in structured exercises with babies and children. These simple techniques build the complex muscles and hand-eye coordination that are vital to their ability to explore and thrive in the world[90].

Saccades

You might think your eyes are still and steady when you look at a fixed object. But the 'window' of your eye - the pupil - is like a camera with a small lens. It can only capture a small portion of the view at any time. So a sub-set of those binocular vision muscles fine-tune your gaze's direction to take a series of snapshots, like an action photographer at a sports event. Your brain even predicts where the eye will need to go next[91].

This prediction is correct in good lighting conditions and with a stable or familiar object in view, so your eyes scroll happily along. But when the lighting or the situation is causing stress - flickering or glaring lights, text that is hard to read or complicated - the accuracy of those jumps goes down, and the number of saccades goes up.

While reading this, your eyes will jump along the sentence around three times per second. In the example below, you may regress over the word 'little' because that collection of letters is relatively unusual. They make a cluster of vertical bars that are harder to read than others, such as the 'rop' in 'drop'. The art and science of typography is a fascinating subject and worth finding more about because the shape, size and colours of words on the page can make the world of difference to a young person's ability to learn to read.

Blinking

The front of your eyes has many nerve endings, which means they are extremely sensitive to scratches or drying out. So the blink reflex works like the screen wash and windscreen wipers on a car to keep the eye's surface moist and clean.

When you blink naturally in a calm and safe environment, your brain feels confident about what will happen next and fills in the time when your eyes are closed. But when a bright light blinds you or you have something in your eye that you want to get rid of, your blink rate goes up.

The problem is that more blinks mean more time when you are effectively blind. That leads to an instant stress response: your heart races and the adrenal glands get to work. As a result, your eyes dart around the scene faster, and each saccade covers a greater distance adding to the strain.

At the other end of the scale, when you focus on a detailed task - typing on a screen or playing a video game, for example - you tend to blink less. This reduced blink rate is one reason students can suffer from painful dry eye or computer vision syndrome. Their risk of suffering from these distressing conditions is made worse when they are dehydrated or taking some medications. That's because these factors lead to changes in the quantity and quality of tear production, so the film dries out more quickly [92].

Blind sight

Scientists have always wondered how people who were completely blind could sometimes perceive shapes and movement - they called it 'blind sight'. They were also intrigued by how blind people could 'tell' when to go to bed. A team in Seattle in the 1980s were amazed to discover that around 5% of the top layer of the retina cells had a secret second life - they were not only working as a relay station for the visual cortex like all the others. They also had a hotline directly to the body clock, alerting and emotion-regulating centres at the top of the brain stem.

They called these special cells intrinsically photosensitive retinal ganglion cells (or ipRCGs) because, unlike the other cells in that top retinal layer, they respond to light in their own right. That intrinsic or independent light response is thanks to the presence of a light-responsive protein called melanopsin [93].

So even when the rods and cones are not working, this top layer of cells keeps reacting to light, particularly 'sky blue' wavelengths. Just like the rods and cones that give us vision, the response is on a curve. It's not an 'on-off' switch: a small amount of light will still generate a signal to the wake-up, mood and attention centres of the brain.

Some people are up to 50 times more sensitive than others, and even for one person, the response changes at different times of the day: 10 lux - roughly the amount of light from a bedside lamp - won't make any difference at all in the morning but can keep your brain awake in the evening.

This parallel system evolved to respond to the amount of ambient light, particularly from the sun in the sky, as a reliable signal of the day- or nighttime and is critical to setting your body clock, mood and attention.

Brain

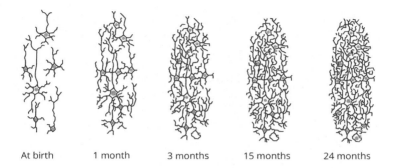

| At birth | 1 month | 3 months | 15 months | 24 months |

Changing number of neural connections from birth to 24 months.

The 'hardware' of vision is remarkable enough. However, the real magic takes place inside your brain.

You can think of the developing brain as a virgin forest. As you take the same route day after day, you will slowly wear a pathway. You might leave a faint trace of your passage the first few times. But over time, this route becomes more established until it becomes an open road you choose without thinking, just as you take a familiar path to work on 'autopilot'.

When you are born, the forest of synaptic connections in your brain is equally lush and overgrown with an almost infinite number of routes you could take. But your brain goes through an intensive 'wiring and firing' process in the first two years of life to build the critical pathways that your environment demands. Scans of a two-year-old's brain show a rich lattice of potential paths, all in the early stages of formation. You will never have as many connections in your brain again. That forest of possibilities goes through a radical spring clean through childhood into adolescence so that we keep only the pathways we use all the time or to build new memories, especially when they have a strong emotional charge[94].

That is why we tend to remember songs and events from our teenage years so vividly - a phenomenon known as the 'reminiscence bump'[95].

Selective vision

Your eyes deliver a constant stream of data to the brain to keep you safe and ensure you're ready to make the most of any opportunity coming over the horizon.

You may be surprised to know that you can 'see' an object in as little as 13 milliseconds, many times faster than your brain can process that information to create conscious 'vision'. That's because signals about fast-moving edges go directly to your brain stem to trigger an immediate response. That's how you can hit a tennis ball before it hits you[96].

But your eyes only gather very simple patterns about edge colour and movement. So if your eyesight is poor, or if you are in an unusual or threatening situation, your brain is going to be hard at work in the background to cross-check the visual cues against signals from your other senses to decide what that information means and whether it's something you need to worry about.

Some default predictions are 'hard wired' from birth - light usually comes from above, and a dark area below an edge usually means a shadow, for example.

But your brain will also compare the visual input with other cues, including sound, taste, scent and touch, to build a picture of reality that you can act upon. You are also using subtle cues you may not be consciously aware of, such as a temperature change and texture variations that might indicate dirt or damage. You may be surprised to learn that, although we typically think of five senses, there are 33 distinct sensory pathways[97]. These include a sense of time passing that your brain tracks using changes in the light and other signals such as heartbeat and hunger.

Children on the autistic spectrum or experiencing anxiety are especially alert to any signs that the visual and non-visual clues do not 'add up'. For example, they tend to find rapid or unexpected change particularly unnerving.

Equally, you can use light to create clear signals, such as a routine change in the colour or brightness of the light to prepare for mealtimes or switch from focused time to relaxation.

Seeing eye to eye

One of the first skills a baby learns is recognising their primary caregiver and reading their expression. This learning happens within the first few hours after birth, long before they can speak or understand language. Most of us can identify between seven and nine expressions based on the eyes alone[98].

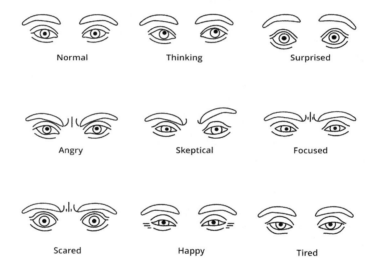

When there is not enough light - or when the contrast is too high- it is much harder to see these vital signs that are so essential when learning how to communicate with other people and understand their feelings.

Light distribution is not only crucial in seeing 'eye to eye'. It is also a powerful signal of your position relative to another person: your brain interprets intense light from behind another person as a signal that the escape route is blocked. This dimension is particularly vital for young children who may feel vulnerable or perhaps even have experienced the trauma of bullying or intimidation from others at school or online.

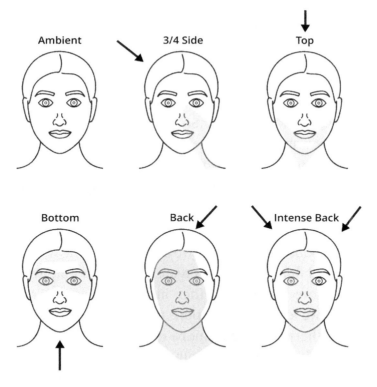

Working out your relationship with someone else using the position of the light.

You can encourage them to be aware of how lighting affects the way they see other people and make choices for themselves to be more comfortable and confident in their interactions with you: use lower-level light sources, wall washers or task lights to see your face clearly and avoid blocking the light which can be seen as threatening. For example, you can guide them to position themselves and adapt the lighting to build rapport with a friend or teacher, even on a video call.

Hue-Heat effect

Another example of using lighting to hack the brain's powerful prediction system is the 'hue-heat' effect. Your brain expects a warm and cosy space will be physically warmer too. So you can feel up to two degrees warmer when the lighting in a room creates a warm and relaxing effect. Equally, lighting that creates a fresh and open feeling is likely to predict a cool temperature without adjusting the thermostat[99].

The cosy campfire glow effect extends to our interactions with others: we see others in a warmer light and find it easier to create and collaborate when we believe we are together in a safe place[100]. As a result, we lose our inhibitions and tend to sit closer to each other[101] consume more calories in an intimate, warmly-lit space[102] . Equally, we are more likely to take more rational and socially-responsible decisions, including healthier food choices, when the lighting suggests an open-air public setting[103]. We even seem to find it easier to broach tough conversations about medical diagnosis and treatment in clinical and hygienic-looking lighting although the effects are subtle and complex[104].

Time-keeping

The discovery of the non-visual pathway and its link to the body clock has helped us to understand the critical role of the natural cycle of bright days and dark nights in the healthy function of every aspect of our bodies and brains. This new field of research, chronobiology, is driving a new generation of lighting solutions that begin to mimic the dynamic qualities that we need to be healthy and happy.

Conclusion

Most of us take our eyes and brain for granted. And yet, together, they drive every single cell in your body and brain every moment of the day and right through the night. Your remarkable eye-brain team has been whirring away in the background since before you were born.

A new science is uncovering the link between our indoor lives and a grim catalogue of physical and mental health conditions. These cast a long shadow over the health and happiness of our precious young people. At the same time, this new understanding is laying the foundations for simple, sustainable and practical solutions and a new generation of energy-efficient lighting technologies. The next chapter will look at these innovations so you can shop confidently.

"There's greatness in smallness. Just look into the eyes of a child."

Dean Henryson

American author and psychotherapist

Further reading

Please use this QR code for links to books and papers.

5/ How lights work

"Great technology is invisible."

Steve Jobs

Entrepreneur and Founder
of Apple Computers

Introduction

T he main aim of this book is to give you a quick introduction to practical techniques and some 'killer arguments' for the young people in your life. Although daylight - and darkness -should always be the first point of call, it's just not practical to be outside as much as we should. So which artificial lights should you buy?

You can probably see at least five lights from the spot where you're sitting right now - even if you're sitting in a car. The average Western adult will own around 40, without counting the dozens of indicators, alarms and screens quietly glowing in the background in every corner of your home, office and garage. Lighting will burn up to 20% of your electricity bill and can turbo-charge the value of your home or office.

And yet shopping for this everyday essential is bewildering and boring. Most of us have no idea what the numbers mean. So we click on a special offer and hope for the best. You may have a drawer full of bulbs that didn't work out for one reason or another but you feel uncomfortable just throwing them away. That's a waste of money. The carbon footprint adds up too.

NASA realised they couldn't afford to leave these decisions to chance either. You may be surprised to discover just how much of that space-age technology is packed into the dull old lightbulbs around you right now. In this chapter, you will learn how lighting technologies work, what to look out for, and how to focus your budget where it counts. You will discover how you can use lighting to save money and even boost the value of your property.

Lighting technologies

Thanks to new laws for energy efficiency, LED lights will soon be the only artificial light sources you can buy. But most of us have no idea what that means.

But the average home in the UK is over 50 years old [105] an average of 35 in the USA. That means that unless you have gone through the expense and disruption of a complete rewire, your home or office combines at least one generation of wiring, switches on the wall and electronic controls - and the lightbulbs. You may even live with a combination of all three.

LED technology can bolt onto your existing system reasonably well. But it generates light radically differently from every other technology that went before. That has a knock-on effect on wiring and controls and even the shape and position of the lights.

So to make sure that you buy the best lightbulbs for the job - and make the most of your investment- it's worth having a quick look at what you already have.

Incandescent lights

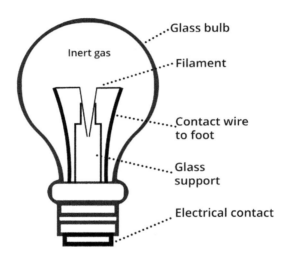

The word incandescent means glowing.

Eddison's remarkable innovation was to drive electric current down a coil of copper wire in a glass bulb under a vacuum. The wire becomes so hot that it glows white. Around 80% of the power is lost in heat, leaving just 20% as useful light.

A thicker wire glows brightly and uses more current or 'Watts'. The legacy of the incandescent system can still be seen on some lighting packages today ('20Watt equivalent', for example).

Incandescent lights draw mains' electricity directly from the wall and squeeze it through the copper wire. The mains power comes down the wire as an alternating wave that goes up and down at around 240 times or cycles per second (or 240Hz). The filament in the light bulb stays hot enough between those cycles for the change to be invisible to the naked eye.

Fluorescent lights

The American giant General Electric pioneered the next generation of lighting, known as fluorescent lighting, in the 1930s. Their research teams harnessed the discovery that a phosphor coating in a magnetic field will make that coating light up or 'fluoresce'. Insects such as fireflies and fish in the depths of the ocean use the same principle known as bioluminescence. They fine-tuned a mechanism to generate that magnetic field with an electrical charge. They then introduced mercury to boost the strength and resilience of the reaction.

Their critical problem was to transform the ebb and flow of alternating current into the constant charge they needed to feed the reaction inside the tube. So engineers built an electronic 'ballast' to gather and release a massive electrical charge into the vacuum chamber to kick-start the reaction. The ballast then continues to buffer and feed charge into the chamber to maintain the smooth supply. Manufacturers spotted a commercial opportunity in the energy-conscious domestic market. So they developed the compact fluorescent, the standard looped version that could be fitted directly into standard light fittings as an eco-friendly upgrade.

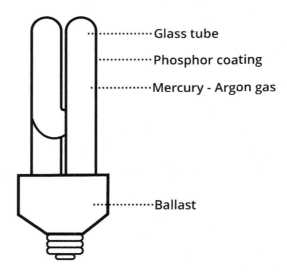

Glass tube
Phosphor coating
Mercury - Argon gas

Ballast

However, over time the electronic components become unreliable and fail. Around 10% of people find this high-speed flicker triggers eye strain and mild headaches. For some people, the consequences can be more severe, including migraine headaches and epilepsy.

When we dump these lamps into landfill, rather than through industry-sponsored recycling programmes, the mercury coating leaches into the soil and groundwater. As a result, these heavy metals build up over time, with devastating effects on plants, animals and aquatic life for decades to come.

LED's

During the 1980s, electronics engineers were looking for a miniature low-energy technique to indicate a circuit's 'on-off' status. They discovered they could engineer the surface of a semiconductor chip to force a shift in the electron's energy state. A charge spins off this reaction as a photon or packet of light. These first light-emitting diodes were tiny single-colour chips in blue, red or green.

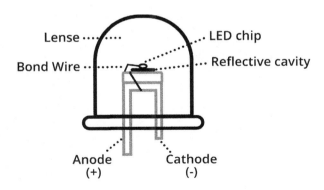

Single-colour LED

You will have dozens of these quietly glowing in your home and office, from the indicator in the fridge to TV standby indicators and the dashboard in your car.

Manufacturers poured billions of dollars into a fiercely competitive race to design a light source that would deliver "white light" that would be bright enough to compete with fluorescent technology at a reasonable cost. Nichia was the first to release a commercial product in 2010. They were the first, but hundreds of others have followed since.

How are LED's made?

The semiconductor chip in the LED is a tiny part of the lightbulb you buy.

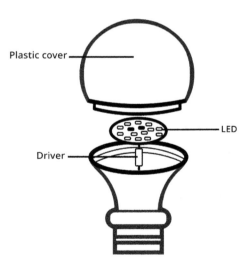

Typical retrofit lightbulb

The rest of the structure is essentially electronics and packaging: switches in the base engineered to feed the current into the chip correctly, reflective lenses to adjust the angle of the beam and a sealed outer coating to protect the delicate connections from dust and moisture.

'Organic' LEDs

The next generation of LEDs builds on the discovery of electroluminescence in organic materials in the 1950s. Two factors drove this innovation. The first is the rising cost and consumer awareness of the carbon footprint involved in traditional LED manufacture. The second is a growing market for lighting in decorative, architectural and other applications where compact profile and flexibility are more important than brightness.

What this new technology means for you

LED technology demands a steady stream of electrons rather than a wave. The engineers again faced the problem of delivering a consistent flow of electrons. The most basic LED products, such as the flexible LED strip, are simply an array of semiconductor chips stuck on a board with printed copper connections. These products need an external driver to transform the alternating mains power into a direct current.

Manufacturers for the domestic market remove the complication of the external drive by packing the electronics into the fitting. Today, most retrofit lightbulbs are a sealed 'plug-and-play' unit that runs directly from the mains power.

Space age technology, steam age designs

There is no practical reason for the LED lightbulb to look anything like the technologies that went before. It doesn't need a vacuum or a gas-filled chamber. The chip draws very little power and only requires two fine copper wires to carry the current. Moreover, the chip is so tiny and emits so little heat that a creative designer can tuck the light source into almost any space.

But the bulk of the market is for replacements. So the new LED products needed to fit into the old lamp holders. That means that old and new lightbulbs might look the same. But the qualities of the light are very different. As a result, they will affect your body and brain in different ways.

Most of us know what to check on the label when we're shopping for healthy food. But we have never learnt what to look out for when it comes to the lights. The following section offers a brief introduction so you know what questions to ask.

"In the right light, at the right time, everything is extraordinary."

Aaron Rose

American film director, artist, exhibition curator and writer

Further reading

Please use this QR code for links to books and papers

6/ Shopping guide

"Price is what you pay.
Value is what you get."

Warren Buffet

American business magnate, investor,
and philanthropist.

I hope you can see why it's worth taking a look at the lights - if only because every time you flip the switch, you are sending a surge of power through a remarkable feat of quantum engineering, light years away from Edison's glowing wire.

You may never have noticed their quiet qualities before. And yet your brain is alive to subtle nuances of colour, flicker and glare. You will be sensing the difference between a space where someone has considered the lighting with care and one where the shades are dusty, the sources are slightly different colours - and perhaps some don't work at all. Children's eyes and brains are so much sharper than ours. The humble lightbulb, hiding in plain sight, is likely to be shaping their experience even more than ours.

And yet, once you start to pay attention, it can be hard to ignore these subtle distractions. You have more control than you imagine. Even small changes will make a world of difference to you and those you love. Whether you want to buy a new or a replacement light, you face a bewildering array of variations, options and prices. Here are some practical tips so you can get the right light for the job.

1/ Make a plan

Before you start shopping, it's worth considering where you spend the most time and how the natural light moves through the space during the day and into the evening. Think about how these can work together with natural daylight to create layers of interest and show off the best features, objects and materials in a room. The colour and texture of paints and other surfaces can completely transform and affect how bright or cosy a space feels.

There are three broad types of artificial light:

- background or ambient, usually overhead or wall light
- task focus- desk or reading lamps or under-cabinet strips or downlight in your kitchen
- decorative - side lamps, spotlights, flexible strips etc.

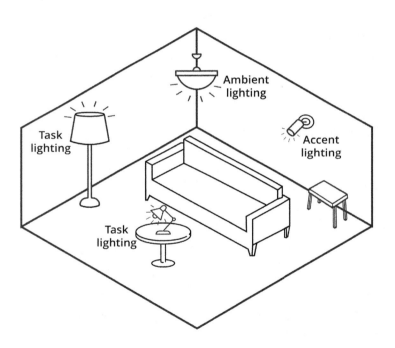

Different types of lighting in the average home.

2/ Narrow down the options

When you're clear on which of the three main types of light you're looking for, it's time to narrow down your options. Here are the essential filters for your search. The lightbulbs should be around for the next 10 years, so it's worth choosing carefully. You might even start to enjoy the process.

Whichever product you choose, it's worth buying one or two lightbulbs from different companies to compare the effect before investing in a set for your child's bedroom, living room, office or hallway.

Even though the specifications may look the same, you may be surprised just how different they can look when you compare them side by side. Consistency is particularly vital in a space where you will be able to see several lights at the same time. Once you start to notice, those minor differences can be really annoying!

3/ Set the filters

Base

If you're looking for a lightbulb to replace an existing one, you need to make sure the base of the new lamp will fit the current lamp holder. The international standard for lightbulb bases uses a letter and a type.

The first letter reflects the type. E = Edison (screw), B = bayonet, GU = General Use.

The numbers represent the diameter or distance (e.g. GU10 = 10mm between the pins on the spotlight base).

Common UK Light Bulb fittings

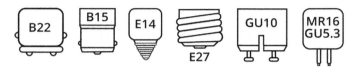

Common US Light Bulb fittings

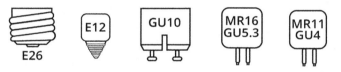

Common lightbulb bases

Power

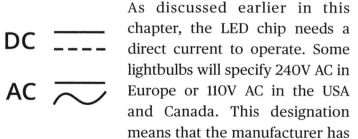

As discussed earlier in this chapter, the LED chip needs a direct current to operate. Some lightbulbs will specify 240V AC in Europe or 110V AC in the USA and Canada. This designation means that the manufacturer has packed the electronics into the base.

Other products will specify direct current or DC: the average LED strip is likely to be 12V or 24V. If the product needs direct current, you will need a driver that is the right size for the lights. Again, a good supplier should have a helpline so you can ask for advice.

Brightness

The basic unit of light is a lux. This is the amount of light that one standard candle would deliver to a white surface measuring one square meter placed one meter away.

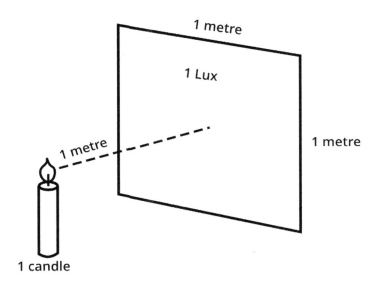

Measuring one lux

But, just as sound fades as you move away from a loudspeaker, the amount of light you get from a light source looks depends on your distance. So there is a difference between the light coming from the lightbulb (lux) and how much reaches your eye or the task (lumens).

There are many free downloadable apps called 'light meters' that you can use on your phone to measure how much light you are getting. As a general rule, aim for around 100 lux for simple tasks, 500 for more detailed work - and up to 1,000, or even 1,500 lux for focused work - in a workshop for example especially if you need glasses.

A second, more technical measurement reflects how much the light source is likely to affect your non-visual system or how many bright blue 'wake-up' wavelengths are in the source. These 'enhanced blue" products are designed to create an alert and wide awake feeling.

Unfortunately, most consumer products do not provide this data. But, as a general rule, lights that look cooler or 'blue' will generally feel brighter and fresher and generate more of the 'sky blue' wavelengths that stimulate the non-visual system.

Dimming

A dimmable product is a simple solution to create different atmospheres with the same source. However, they are generally more expensive because they use more sophisticated electronics.

Any LED should work with most dimmer switches. But you may notice a flicker and a buzzing sound, especially when the lights are on the dimmest setting.

That is because of the fundamental difference in the way incandescent, fluorescent and LED lights use electricity.

Older technologies need a lot of power to generate light. But they still work perfectly well even if the supply is unstable.

By contrast, an LED needs very little electricity. But they do demand far greater precision because the semiconductor chip needs a steady and stable supply of electrons to work correctly and last a long time. That is especially important when you are dimming because the most basic LEDs do this by switching on and off very fast.

The other factor is the amount of power that the circuit will draw. Dimmers for incandescent lights were engineered to cope with large amounts of electricity. In contrast, the average LED takes up to 90% less. That means you will need a new dimmer switch for your new lights to keep them working well for their entire rated life and deliver a smooth range of brightnesses from 0 to 100%.

So when you replace an incandescent or fluorescent light source with a dimmable LED, you may need to replace the switches.

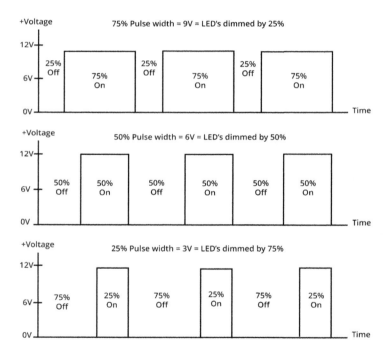

Dimming an LED light source

Most major lightbulb manufacturers will have a place on their website or a technical helpline to guide you to a compatible dimmer switch: it's in their interest because a mismatched light will flicker and burn hot - and burn out years before the rated lifetime.

Choosing the correct brightness for the situation can be more straightforward and more environmentally friendly rather than paying for the extra complication and potential headache of a dimmable version.

Colour temperature

Colour temperature	2,000 K - 3,000 K	3,100 K 4,500 K	4,600 K - 6,500 K
Light appearance	Warm white	Cool white	Daylight
Ambience	Cozy, calm, inviting, intimate	Bright, vibrant	Crisp, invigorarting
Best for	Pendant lights, restaurant and residential ambient lighting, table and floor lamps	Garages, general classroom and offices, task lighting	Display and focus lighting, security, clinical settings

Typical colour temperatures and where you might use them.

Some lights will look slightly yellowish, while others will look slightly blue.

133

You may see the words 'warm', daylight' or 'cool' on the packaging or a number followed by the letter 'K'. That stands for 'Kelvin', the international unit for colour temperature. The higher the number, the cooler or bluer the light source will appear. One easy way to remember is that metal glows orange when first heated up but will become white hot at a higher temperature.

Choose daylight or cool for a fresh open-air feeling and warm lights for a soft, warm atmosphere. A growing number of manufacturers produce amber or 'antique' lamps. These are rated around 1800k and often use a warm chip and an orange coating or filter. These can be an excellent option for ambient evening and night lights.

You may find that lightbulbs with the same 'colour temperature' from different manufacturers look surprisingly different, resulting in an uneven or patchy look. If you are a perfectionist, consider buying all the lightbulbs for a given space from the same place.

Colour rendering

Your brain can't "tell" which wavelengths are in a light source, in the same way, that you can't always identify every ingredient in a dish. That's because the visual cortex blends visible and invisible radiation to generate our sense of a white light. However, while all incandescent light sources generate a balanced blend of wavelengths, LED sources do not.

That's because each manufacturer will design the coatings on their chip to create their unique blend of wavelengths. That means that two light sources might "look" the same but are composed of a different 'recipe' of wavelengths.

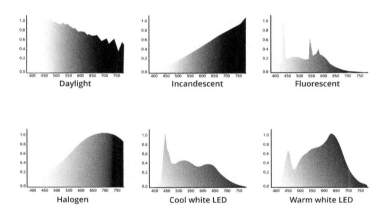

Balance of wavelengths in typical light sources used at home.

The individual phosphors will fade and change over time. So even if two light sources started out looking the same, they will change colour and brightness in slightly different ways.

Colour Rendering Index, or 'CRI', is the primary industry standard measure of the range of wavelengths that the light source gives out. In principle, the higher the number, the closer the light source will be to 'natural sunlight'. So choose a CRI greater than 90 for spaces where you will spend a lot of time, and aim for around CRI 80 for utility and storage areas. Other measures include the 'R-value, describing the colour quality in more detail.

Most manufacturers will focus on the R9 value that measures how well you can see red tones. The quality of red tones is critical in spaces where you want to communicate clearly: schools for students with learning difficulties, for example. That's because the blood flow around your face changes with your emotions, leading to subtle changes in your colouring.

You may think that colour rendering is a minor detail. But research suggests that higher colour rendering can have a surprisingly powerful effect, reducing stress, improving mood, and even improving sleep.

Colour changing

LED engines are so small and easy to control that manufacturers can pack several coloured chips into the same fitting. You can see the array on flexible strips, for example.

The key to choosing a product that will last is the quality and reliability of the controls. For example, some rely on your domestic wifi connection, while others use an independent signalling system. In addition, many manufacturers' products will only work with their own branded app, leaving you vulnerable to their financial model, privacy and upgrade policy: check how they harvest your data and whether they are likely to demand payments through a subscription arrangement, for example.

It is also good to check that the supplier offers after-sales support with a helpline and a guaranteed returns policy with free postage. Unfortunately, I have found that some of the cheaper products only provide a printed leaflet that is almost impossible to read, so you are stuck if there is a problem.

Beam angle

This number describes the shape of the cone of light generated by the light source. For example, a spotlight may deliver 15 degrees, while a lightbulb without shielding can create a wide spread of light up to 260 degrees. Choosing the right beam angle is most important for places where you will sit to read or work. That's because not only will it help you to direct the light where you need it. Choosing the right beam angle will also help to make sure you aren't blinded by glare.

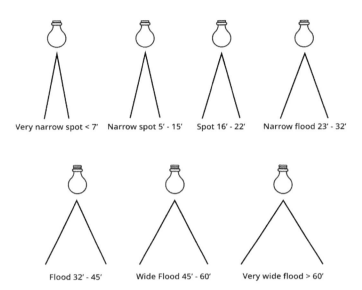

Very narrow spot < 7'   Narrow spot 5' - 15'   Spot 16' - 22'   Narrow flood 23' - 32'

Flood 32' - 45'   Wide Flood 45' - 60'   Very wide flood > 60'

Typical beam angles

Other things to look out for

- Glare rating - this is an industry measure of how well-shielded the light source is - for example whether it has a diffuser that spreads the light out more evenly, or has a shade or shield that blocks the light. Of course, whether a light source is uncomfortable will depend on where you are sitting relative to the light source and other reflective surfaces such as windows and picture frames. The only way to really tell is to experiment at home when

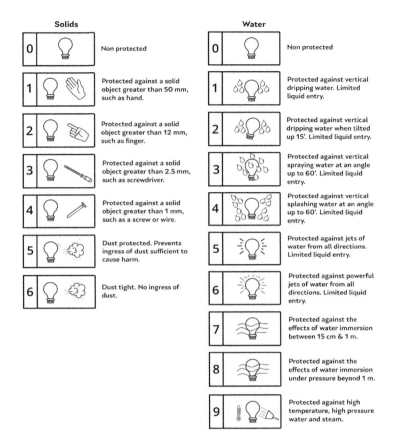

Solids				Water		
0		Non protected		0		Non protected
1		Protected against a solid object greater than 50 mm, such as hand.		1		Protected against vertical dripping water. Limited liquid entry.
2		Protected against a solid object greater than 12 mm, such as finger.		2		Protected against vertical dripping water when tilted up 15'. Limited liquid entry.
3		Protected against a solid object greater than 2.5 mm, such as screwdriver.		3		Protected against vertical spraying water at an angle up to 60'. Limited liquid entry.
4		Protected against a solid object greater than 1 mm, such as a screw or wire.		4		Protected against vertical splashing water at an angle up to 60'. Limited liquid entry.
5		Dust protected. Prevents ingress of dust sufficient to cause harm.		5		Protected against jets of water from all directions. Limited liquid entry.
6		Dust tight. No ingress of dust.		6		Protected against powerful jets of water from all directions. Limited liquid entry.
				7		Protected against the effects of water immersion between 15 cm & 1 m.
				8		Protected against the effects of water immersion under pressure beyond 1 m.
				9		Protected against high temperature, high pressure water and steam.

What IP ratings mean

you're sitting in different positions or walking into the space.

- Lumens per watt - the amount of light you get from the amount of power you put in.

- Lifetime rating - how many hours a lightbulb will last - as a guide, a 100,000-hour rated lightbulb should last five years at eight hours per day. This is hard to check because life depends partly on where you have installed the light. Other conditions, including the quality of switches and dimmers can make a product fail more quickly.

- Ecodesign Directive - New EU rule that says that manufacturers must design all new light sources so that a reasonably skilled person can repair them.

- WEEE - Waste Electronic and Electrical Equipment regulations - shows that the company contributes to a nationwide scheme to recycle electrical products responsibly, while other safety marks - BSI, CE etc. - show the product is safe.

- Protection or 'IP' rating - the first number is whether solid objects can get in, and the second is whether water can get in. This is especially important in spaces where children will be left unattended.

Save money

Making all these decisions may seem like hard work. It may sound more expensive too.

Better-quality products can often cost more up-front than the 'budget' alternatives and the cost of professional advice - maybe even an electrician to upgrade the switches too. Investing in an upgrade may mean spending time shopping around and asking for professional advice. You may need to call in an electrician to install dimmers and sensors. But shopping wisely can save you money. It can even help boost the value of your home or office. It's worth setting the extra cost in context, too. According to a recent report[106], the average parent in the UK will spend over £28,000 per child on extracurricular activities while living at home. But, as I hope you have seen, the right light at the right time can help ensure they can make the most of all those excellent opportunities.

Here are some simple tips that will help you to focus your budget where it will add the most value.

Sunlight

Make sure you take advantage of natural light during the day. Open your curtains and blinds to let in as much natural light as possible. Use reflective surfaces, such as white walls or mirrors, to distribute light evenly throughout a room. That can increase a room's brightness by up to 20% - and reduce the amount of artificial light you need[107]. It's worth ensuring the windows and fittings are clean, too: Dirty light fixtures can reduce the amount of light they give out and create a gloomy and uncared-for atmosphere[108].

Energy in use

LEDs use up to 80% less energy than incandescent lights and around 20% less than fluorescent technologies. That can lead to significant savings. The other advantage of LEDs is that you can adjust the brightness to the level you need, which cuts energy use too.

Focus light where you need it.

Divide your home into different areas, each with its own lighting needs. Task lighting will deliver the light you need for tasks such as reading or working at a desk. Using separate switches and dimmers for each area will ensure you're productive and comfortable and can help you save money too. It's easy to forget to turn off lights when you leave a room: as a parent, you want to be doing something other than nagging all the time. Motion sensors can be a good solution, especially for outdoor lights. Timers are another simple option, particularly for hallways and porches where you want to create a welcoming impression or improve security at specific times.

Increase curb appeal

Thoughtful lighting can even increase the value of your property.

Layering can create a more dynamic and distinctive look. You can achieve this simply with overhead, table, floor, and accent lighting for artwork, sculptures, or other decorative elements. The colour temperature of your lighting will also alter the look and feel of the space. Make sure all the lights in an area match to create a coherent impression.

Lighting can also highlight architectural features such as a beautiful staircase or a unique ceiling design. A striking statement light or chandelier can add drama and visual interest. Outdoor lighting on pathways and landscape features can help your home to stand out. But exterior lighting needs to be focused and shielded to avoid light pollution and wasted energy.

Upgrading to smart lighting technology, particularly when integrated with home entertainment and security systems can even increase the value of your property.[109] [110].

Conclusion

Shopping for the right lights can feel like a daunting task. But if you focus on the parts of your home or office where you spend most time and take it slowly, you will start to see the difference - and perhaps even enjoy the process!

"Don't short-change yourself when it comes to investing in your own better future."

Jim Rohn

American Author and Motivational Speaker

7/ Conclusion

Y ou have a natural feeling for light. You know instinctively when a space lifts you up or drags you down. You know how a ray of sunshine after rain can transform your day. As a parent, you also know how much a good night's sleep and a moment together in the fresh air can help your chid's eyes sparkle with laughter and their brains relax so they can play and learn. Yet, you know it's not always possible to spend time outside, especially through the long winter months or in the blistering heat of summer.

You already do everything in your power to give them the best start in life: what can be more important than that? And yet most of us never take a moment to notice the one thing that can transform their health and happiness so easily and affordably.

A new science of light, optimised to support life in galaxies far beyond our own, offers proven down-to-earth solutions if we only take a moment to look around. For the first time in history, we understand how light affects our brain and have affordable, effective and sustainable solutions that mean you can do something about it today.

The secret to feeling energised, happier and confident is not rocket science. It is all around you right now. You are a born expert and have everything you need to take control for yourself and those you love.

"View your health as an investment, not an expense."

John Quelch

Author, Harvard Business School Professor

About the Author

Dr Shelley James is an international expert on light and well-being, TEDx and keynote speaker, WELL Advisor, WELL Faculty and Consultant to the Design Age Institute at the Royal College of Art. She is also a glass artist, electrician and open water swimmer and proud godmother, aunt and great-aunt to a growing band of remarkable young people.

Current include global lighting and technology brands, regulators, healthcare and education trusts, architects and designers, academic institutions and museums. A recent social media campaign to raise awareness of the impact of light on teens reached over 2.5 million young people around the world. Her TEDx talk was in the top three in the world in the month following its release.

Index

A

Adolescents, 101

Anxiety, 19, 40, 49, 58, 75, 86-87, 122

B

Babies, 15, 69, 108, 113, 115-116

Binocular Vision, 115-116

Blue light, 13, 23, 33, 43, 51

Body Clock, 10-14, 29-30, 32-35, 42-44, 46-47, 51-53, 58, 62, 89, 99, 101, 107, 119, 126

C

Cancer, 74

Central Pacemaker, 11, 33

Chronotype, 37, 89

Circadian, 29, 32, 35, 46

Colour Vision, 112-113

Coloured filters, 97

D

Dawn Simulator, 57, 68

Dementia, 15

Depression, 19, 45, 56, 58-59, 63-64, 75, 77

Dopamine, 62, 76

F

Fluorescent, 132-133, 135

H

Hue-Heat Effect, 125

I

Incandescent, 131-132

ipRGC, 112-113

Iris, 21, 108-109

L

Light Pollution, 45

Lightbulb Bases, 142-143

M

Melatonin, 33-34, 43-44, 51, 99

Memory Palace, 85, 95, 102

Metabolism, 10, 41

Mood, 19, 32, 49-50, 57-59, 62-67, 69, 72, 74-75, 78, 89, 96, 98-99, 119

N

Naps, 32

Nighttime, 119

P

Protege Effect, 90

R

Retina, 110-112, 118

S

SAD, 57, 63, 67-68, 76, 78

Screens, 34, 43, 45, 51-52, 91, 103, 105, 111, 115, 129

Serotonin, 62, 76, 89

Shopping, 7, 20, 27, 72, 129, 137, 139-141, 143

Space station, 14, 20

Sunlight, 23-24, 42, 47, 63, 67-70, 72-74, 76, 82, 89, 99

Sunscreen, 68-71

T

Teens, 16, 26, 29, 41, 46-47, 52, 58

U

UV, 68-72

Bibliography

[1] Hu, J., Shi, Y., Zhang, J., Huang, X., Wang, Q., Zhao, H., Shen, J., Chen, Z., Song, W., Zheng, P., Zhan, S., Sun, Y., Cai, P., An, K., Ouyang, C., Zhao, B., Zhou, Q., Xu, L., Xiong, W., . . . Xue, T. (2022). Melanopsin retinal ganglion cells mediate light-promoted brain development. *Cell*, *185*(17), 3124-3137.e3115. https://doi.org/10.1016/j.cell.2022.07.009

[2] Domagalik, A., Oginska, H., Beldzik, E., Fafrowicz, M., Pokrywka, M., Chaniecki, P., Rekas, M., & Marek, T. (2020). Long-Term Reduction of Short-Wavelength Light Affects Sustained Attention and Visuospatial Working Memory With No Evidence for a Change in Circadian Rhythmicity. *Front Neurosci*, *14*, 654. https://doi.org/10.3389/fnins.2020.00654

[3] Houser, K., Boyce, P., Zeitzer, J., & Herf, M. (2021). Human-centric lighting: Myth, magic or metaphor? *Lighting Research & Technology*, *53*(2), 97-118. https://doi.org/10.1177/1477153520958448

[4] Douma, L. G., & Gumz, M. L. (2018). Circadian clock-mediated regulation of blood pressure. *Free Radic Biol Med*, *119*, 108-114. https://doi.org/10.1016/j.freeradbiomed.2017.11.024

[5] Scott, E. M. (2015). Circadian clocks, obesity and cardiometabolic function. *Diabetes Obes Metab*, *17 Suppl 1*, 84-89. https://doi.org/10.1111/dom.12518

[6] Trošt Bobić, T., Šečić, A., Zavoreo, I., Matijević, V., Filipović, B., Kolak, Ž., Bašić Kes, V., Ciliga, D., & Sajković, D. (2016). The Impact of Sleep Deprivation on the Brain. *Acta Clin Croat*, *55*(3), 469-473. https://doi.org/10.20471/acc.2016.55.03.17

[7] Sabia S, Dugravot A, Léger D, Ben Hassen C, Kivimaki M, Singh-Manoux A (2022) Association of sleep duration at age 50, 60, and 70 years with risk of multimorbidity in the UK: 25-year follow-up of the Whitehall II cohort study. PLoS Med 19(10): e1004109. https://doi.org/10.1371/journal.pmed.1004109

[8] https://www.iarc.who.int/news-events/iarc-monographs-volume-124-night-shift-work/

[9] Ticleanu, C. (2021). Impacts of home lighting on human health. *Lighting Research & Technology*, *53*(5), 453-475. https://doi.org/10.1177/14771535211021064

[10] https://ledhut.co.uk/blogs/news/the-brighter-britain-report-how-lighting-impacts-our-lives

[11] https://www.commonsensemedia.org/research/technology-addiction-concern-controversy-and-finding-balance

[12] https://www.commonsensemedia.org/sites/default/files/research/report/2016_csm_technology_addiction_executive_summary.pdf

[13] Tandon, P. S., Zhou, C., & Christakis, D. A. (2012). Frequency of Parent-Supervised Outdoor Play of US Preschool-Aged Children. *Archives of Pediatrics & Adolescent Medicine*, *166*(8), 707-712. https://doi.org/10.1001/archpediatrics.2011.1835

[14] https://natureofamericans.org/findings/topic-summary/adults

[15] https://www.buildingh.org/survey-research

[16] https://www.unodc.org/pdf/criminal_justice/ UN_Standard_Minimum_Rules_for_the_Treatment_ of_Prisoners.pdf

[17] https://ageoflightinnovations.com/2021/06/dr-james-greenberg-dr-richard-lang-robert-soler/

[18] https://ageoflightinnovations.com/2022/08/ interview-with-simon-smith-sweyne-park-school/

[19] https://ageoflightinnovations.com/2022/08/erik-askensjo/

[20] https://ageoflightinnovations.com/2021/06/ed-russell/

[21] Geoffroy, P. A., Schroder, C. M., Reynaud, E., & Bourgin, P. (2019). Efficacy of light therapy versus antidepressant drugs, and of the combination versus monotherapy, in major depressive episodes: A systematic review and meta-analysis. *Sleep Med Rev*, *48*, 101213. https://doi.org/10.1016/ j.smrv.2019.101213

[22] Okano, K., Kaczmarzyk, J. R., Dave, N., Gabrieli, J. D. E., & Grossman, J. C. (2019). Sleep quality, duration, and consistency are associated with better academic performance in college students. *npj Science of Learning*, *4*(1), 16. https://doi.org/10.1038/s41539-019-0055-z

[23] https://whc.unesco.org/en/list/491/

[24] Tekiner, H. (2014). Aretaeus of cappadocia and his treatises on diseases. *Turkish Neurosurgery*. https://doi.org/10.5137/1019-5149.jtn.12347-14.0

[25] https://www.ecolenaturopathie.fr/the-symbolism-of-colors-in-ayurveda/?lang=en

[26] Cocilovo, A. (1999). Colored light therapy: overview of its history, theory, recent developments and clinical applications combined with acupuncture. Am J Acupunct, 27(1-2), 71-83.

[27] Evans, R. (2020). Books: Chasing the Sun: The New Science of Sunlight and How it Shapes Our Bodies and Minds: Let There be Light. *Br J Gen Pract*, *70*(691), 80. https://doi.org/10.3399/bjgp20X707957

[28] Ma, A., & Narwold, A. (2019). Which Way is Up? Orientation and Residential Property Values. *Journal of Sustainable Real Estate, 11*(1), 40-59. https://doi.org/10.22300/1949-8276.11.1.40

[29] Sabia, S., Dugravot, A., Léger, D., Ben Hassen, C., Kivimaki, M., & Singh-Manoux, A. (2022). Association of sleep duration at age 50, 60, and 70 years with risk of multimorbidity in the UK: 25-year follow-up of the Whitehall II cohort study. *PLOS Medicine, 19*(10), e1004109. https://doi.org/10.1371/journal.pmed.1004109

[30] Stevens, R. G., Hansen, J., Costa, G., Haus, E., Kauppinen, T., Aronson, K. J., Castaño-Vinyals, G., Davis, S., Frings-Dresen, M. H., Fritschi, L., Kogevinas, M., Kogi, K., Lie, J. A., Lowden, A., Peplonska, B., Pesch, B., Pukkala, E., Schernhammer, E., Travis, R. C., . . . Straif, K. (2011). Considerations of circadian impact for defining 'shift work' in cancer studies: IARC Working Group Report. *Occup Environ Med, 68*(2), 154-162. https://doi.org/10.1136/oem.2009.053512

31 Zhou, Y., Chen, Q., Luo, X., Li, L., Ru, T., & Zhou, G. (2021). Does Bright Light Counteract the Post-lunch Dip in Subjective States and Cognitive Performance Among Undergraduate Students? *Front Public Health, 9,* 652849. https://doi.org/10.3389/fpubh.2021.652849

32 Ticleanu, C. (2021). Impacts of home lighting on human health. *Lighting Research & Technology, 53*(5), 453-475. https://doi.org/10.1177/14771535211021064

33 Fasciani, I., Petragnano, F., Aloisi, G., Marampon, F., Rossi, M., Coppolino, M., Rossi, R., Longoni, B., Scarselli, M., & Maggio, R. (2020). A New Threat to Dopamine Neurons: The Downside of Artificial Light. *Neuroscience, 432.* https://doi.org/10.1016/j.neuroscience.2020.02.047

34 Short MA, Gradisar M, Wright H, Lack LC, Dohnt H, Carskadon MA. Time for bed: parent-set bedtimes associated with improved sleep and daytime functioning in adolescents. Sleep. 2011 Jun 1;34(6):797-800. doi: 10.5665/SLEEP.1052. PMID: 21629368; PMCID: PMC3098947

35 Short, M. A., Booth, S. A., Omar, O., Ostlundh, L., & Arora, T. (2020). The relationship between sleep duration and mood in adolescents: A systematic review and meta-analysis. *Sleep Med Rev*, *52*, 101311. https://doi.org/10.1016/j.smrv.2020.101311

36 Smyth, J. M., Johnson, J. A., Auer, B. J., Lehman, E., Talamo, G., & Sciamanna, C. N. (2018). Online Positive Affect Journaling in the Improvement of Mental Distress and Well-Being in General Medical Patients With Elevated Anxiety Symptoms: A Preliminary Randomized Controlled Trial. *JMIR Mental Health*, *5*(4), e11290. https://doi.org/10.2196/11290

37 Okano, K., Kaczmarzyk, J. R., Dave, N., Gabrieli, J. D. E., & Grossman, J. C. (2019). Sleep quality, duration, and consistency are associated with better academic performance in college students. *npj Science of Learning*, *4*(1), 16. https://doi.org/10.1038/s41539-019-0055-z

[38] Charest, J., & Grandner, M. A. (2020). Sleep and Athletic Performance: Impacts on Physical Performance, Mental Performance, Injury Risk and Recovery, and Mental Health. *Sleep Med Clin*, *15*(1), 41-57. https://doi.org/10.1016/j.jsmc.2019.11.005

[39] van der Helm, E., Gujar, N., & Walker, M. P. (2010). Sleep deprivation impairs the accurate recognition of human emotions. *Sleep*, *33*(3), 335-342. https://doi.org/10.1093/sleep/33.3.335

[40] Gooley, J. J., Chamberlain, K., Smith, K. A., Khalsa, S. B., Rajaratnam, S. M., Van Reen, E., Zeitzer, J. M., Czeisler, C. A., & Lockley, S. W. (2011). Exposure to room light before bedtime suppresses melatonin onset and shortens melatonin duration in humans. *J Clin Endocrinol Metab*, *96*(3), E463-472. https://doi.org/10.1210/jc.2010-2098

41 Tam, S. K. E., Brown, L. A., Wilson, T. S., Tir, S., Fisk, A. S., Pothecary, C. A., van der Vinne, V., Foster, R. G., Vyazovskiy, V. V., Bannerman, D. M., Harrington, M. E., & Peirson, S. N. (2021). Dim light in the evening causes coordinated realignment of circadian rhythms, sleep, and short-term memory. *Proceedings of the National Academy of Sciences, 118*(39), e2101591118. https://doi.org/doi:10.1073/pnas.2101591118

42 Münch, M., Nowozin, C., Regente, J., Bes, F., De Zeeuw, J., Hädel, S., Wahnschaffe, A., & Kunz, D. (2016). Blue-Enriched Morning Light as a Countermeasure to Light at the Wrong Time: Effects on Cognition, Sleepiness, Sleep, and Circadian Phase. *Neuropsychobiology, 74*(4), 207-218. https://doi.org/10.1159/000477093

43 Geoffroy, P. A. (2020). The Light of Hope in Antidepressant Strategies. *Chronobiol Med, 2*(2), 57-60. https://doi.org/10.33069/cim.2020.0008

44 Penckofer, S., Kouba, J., Byrn, M., & Estwing Ferrans, C. (2010). Vitamin D and depression: where is all the sunshine? *Issues Ment Health Nurs, 31*(6), 385-393. https://doi.org/10.3109/01612840903437657

[45] https://www.allaboutvision.com/en-gb/digital-eye-strain/children-computer-vision-syndrome/#:~:text=Go%20outdoors.,risk%20of%20becoming%20short%20sighted! Accessed 29 June 2023.

[46] Veitch, J. A., Stokkermans, M. G. M., & Newsham, G. R. (2013). Linking Lighting Appraisals to Work Behaviors. *Environment and Behavior*, *45*(2), 198-214. https://doi.org/10.1177/0013916511420560

[47] Kwon, M., Remøy, H., Dobbelsteen, A., & Knaack, U. (2018). Personal control and environmental user satisfaction in office buildings: Results of case studies in the Netherlands. *Building and Environment*. https://doi.org/10.1016/j.buildenv.2018.12.021

[48] Ahakwa, I., Yang, J., Agba Tackie, E., & Atingabili, S. (2021). The Influence of Employee Engagement, Work Environment and Job Satisfaction on Organizational Commitment and Performance of Employees: A Sampling Weights in PLS path Modelling. *SEISENSE Journal of Management*, *4*(3), 34-62. https://doi.org/10.33215/sjom.v4i3.641

[49] Thompson, A., Jones, H., Gregson, W., & Atkinson, G. (2014). Effects of dawn simulation on markers of sleep inertia and post-waking performance in humans. *Eur J Appl Physiol*, *114*(5), 1049-1056. https://doi.org/10.1007/s00421-014-2831-z

[50] Rueter, K., Jones, A. P., Siafarikas, A., Chivers, P., Prescott, S. L., & Palmer, D. J. (2021). The Influence of Sunlight Exposure and Sun Protecting Behaviours on Allergic Outcomes in Early Childhood. *Int J Environ Res Public Health*, *18*(10). https://doi.org/10.3390/ijerph18105429

[51] Andrews, D. Q., Rauhe, K., Burns, C., Spilman, E., Temkin, A. M., Perrone-Gray, S., Naidenko, O. V., & Leiba, N. (2022). Laboratory testing of sunscreens on the US market finds lower in vitro SPF values than on labels and even less UVA protection. *Photodermatology, Photoimmunology & Photomedicine*, *38*(3), 224-232. https://doi.org/https://doi.org/10.1111/phpp.12738

[52] Backes, C., Religi, A., Moccozet, L., Behar-Cohen, F., Vuilleumier, L., Bulliard, J. L., & Vernez, D. (2019). Sun exposure to the eyes: predicted UV protection effectiveness of various sunglasses. *J Expo Sci Environ Epidemiol, 29*(6), 753-764. https://doi.org/10.1038/s41370-018-0087-0

[53] Ceban, F., Nogo, D., Carvalho, I. P., Lee, Y., Nasri, F., Xiong, J., Lui, L. M. W., Subramaniapillai, M., Gill, H., Liu, R. N., Joseph, P., Teopiz, K. M., Cao, B., Mansur, R. B., Lin, K., Rosenblat, J. D., Ho, R. C., & McIntyre, R. S. (2021). Association Between Mood Disorders and Risk of COVID-19 Infection, Hospitalization, and Death: A Systematic Review and Meta-analysis. *JAMA Psychiatry, 78*(10), 1079-1091. https://doi.org/10.1001/jamapsychiatry.2021.1818

54 Smyth, J. M., Johnson, J. A., Auer, B. J., Lehman, E., Talamo, G., & Sciamanna, C. N. (2018). Online Positive Affect Journaling in the Improvement of Mental Distress and Well-Being in General Medical Patients With Elevated Anxiety Symptoms: A Preliminary Randomized Controlled Trial. *JMIR Mental Health, 5*(4), e11290. https://doi.org/10.2196/11290

55 Achterbergh, L., Pitman, A., Birken, M., Pearce, E., Sno, H., & Johnson, S. (2020). The experience of loneliness among young people with depression: a qualitative meta-synthesis of the literature. *BMC Psychiatry, 20*(1), 415. https://doi.org/10.1186/s12888-020-02818-3

56 Brent, L. J., Chang, S. W., Gariépy, J. F., & Platt, M. L. (2014). The neuroethology of friendship. *Ann N Y Acad Sci, 1316*(1), 1-17. https://doi.org/10.1111/nyas.12315

57 Lazzerini Ospri, L., Prusky, G., & Hattar, S. (2017). Mood, the Circadian System, and Melanopsin Retinal Ganglion Cells. *Annu Rev Neurosci, 40*, 539-556. https://doi.org/10.1146/annurev-neuro-072116-031324

[58] Lazzerini Ospri, L., Prusky, G., & Hattar, S. (2017). Mood, the Circadian System, and Melanopsin Retinal Ganglion Cells. *Annu Rev Neurosci, 40*, 539-556. https://doi.org/10.1146/annurev-neuro-072116-031324

[59] Schielke, T. (2019). The Language of Lighting: Applying Semiotics in the Evaluation of Lighting Design. *LEUKOS, 15*(2-3), 227-248. https://doi.org/10.1080/15502724.2018.1518715

[60] Morales-Bravo, J., & Navarrete-Hernandez, P. (2022). Enlightening wellbeing in the home: The impact of natural light design on perceived happiness and sadness in residential spaces. *Building and Environment, 223*, 109317. https://doi.org/https://doi.org/10.1016/j.buildenv.2022.109317

[61] Brink, H. W., Loomans, M. G. L. C., Mobach, M. P., & Kort, H. S. M. (2021). Classrooms' indoor environmental conditions affecting the academic achievement of students and teachers in higher education: A systematic literature review. *Indoor Air, 31*(2), 405-425. https://doi.org/https://doi.org/10.1111/ina.12745

[62] Buckley, J., Schneider, M., & Shang, Y. (2005). Fix It and They Might Stay: School Facility Quality and Teacher Retention in Washington, D.C. *Teachers College Record - TEACH COLL REC, 107,* 1107-1123. https://doi.org/10.1111/ j.1467-9620.2005.00506.x

[63] Llinares, C., Castilla, N., & Higuera-Trujillo, J. L. (2021). Do Attention and Memory Tasks Require the Same Lighting? A Study in University Classrooms. *Sustainability, 13*(15), 8374. https:// www.mdpi.com/2071-1050/13/15/8374

[64] Ayala, V., Martínez-Bebia, M., Latorre, J. A., Gimenez-Blasi, N., Jimenez-Casquet, M. J., Conde-Pipo, J., Bach-Faig, A., & Mariscal-Arcas, M. (2021). Influence of circadian rhythms on sports performance. *Chronobiol Int, 38*(11), 1522-1536. https://doi.org/10.1080/07420528.2021.1933003

[65] Yang, B. W., Razo, J., & Persky, A. M. (2019). Using Testing as a Learning Tool. *Am J Pharm Educ, 83*(9), 7324. https://doi.org/10.5688/ ajpe7324

66 Okano, K., Kaczmarzyk, J. R., Dave, N., Gabrieli, J. D. E., & Grossman, J. C. (2019). Sleep quality, duration, and consistency are associated with better academic performance in college students. *npj Science of Learning*, *4*(1), 16. https://doi.org/10.1038/s41539-019-0055-z

67 Tabibian, B., Upadhyay, U., De, A., Zarezade, A., Schölkopf, B., & Gomez-Rodriguez, M. (2019). Enhancing human learning via spaced repetition optimization. *Proceedings of the National Academy of Sciences*, *116*(10), 3988-3993. https://doi.org/doi:10.1073/pnas.1815156116

68 Gaspar, J. M., Christie, G. J., Prime, D. J., Jolicœur, P., & McDonald, J. J. (2016). Inability to suppress salient distractors predicts low visual working memory capacity. *Proceedings of the National Academy of Sciences*, *113*(13), 3693-3698. https://doi.org/doi:10.1073/pnas.1523471113

69 Cutting, J. E., & Armstrong, K. L. (2016). Facial expression, size, and clutter: Inferences from movie structure to emotion judgments and back. *Atten Percept Psychophys*, *78*(3), 891-901. https://doi.org/10.3758/s13414-015-1003-5

[70] Wagner, I. C., Konrad, B. N., Schuster, P., Weisig, S., Repantis, D., Ohla, K., Kühn, S., Fernández, G., Steiger, A., Lamm, C., Czisch, M., & Dresler, M. (2021). Durable memories and efficient neural coding through mnemonic training using the method of loci. *Science Advances, 7*(10), eabc7606. https://doi.org/ doi:10.1126/sciadv.abc7606

[71] Stevenson, M. P., Schilhab, T., & Bentsen, P. (2018). Attention Restoration Theory II: a systematic review to clarify attention processes affected by exposure to natural environments. *Journal of Toxicology and Environmental Health, Part B, 21*(4), 227-268. https://doi.org/ 10.1080/10937404.2018.1505571

[72] Ghahremani, M., Smith, E. E., Chen, H.-Y., Creese, B., Goodarzi, Z., & Ismail, Z. (2023). Vitamin D supplementation and incident dementia: Effects of sex, APOE, and baseline cognitive status. *Alzheimer's & Dementia: Diagnosis, Assessment & Disease Monitoring, 15*(1), e12404. https://doi.org/https://doi.org/10.1002/ dad2.12404

[73] Alkhudairy, Z., & Al Shamlan, F. (2022). The Use of Chromagen Lenses in Different Ocular and Non-ocular Conditions: A Prospective Cohort Study. *Cureus, 14*(9), e28963. https://doi.org/10.7759/cureus.28963

[74] Abdi, F., Amjadi, M. A., Zaheri, F., & Rahnemaei, F. A. (2021). Role of vitamin D and calcium in the relief of primary dysmenorrhea: a systematic review. *Obstet Gynecol Sci, 64*(1), 13-26. https://doi.org/10.5468/ogs.20205

[75] Cox, D. A. (2021, 3 July 2023). The College Connection: The Education Divide in American Social and Community Life. https://www.americansurveycenter.org/research/the-college-connection-the-education-divide-in-american-social-and-community-life/?mkt_tok=NDc1LVBCUSO5NzEAAAGBWFLE4HQ2MtOOYKmHoljQ6QWQz7Y4x0OOzcOL1OTR-f_-kaFYDbc7vS-xvlOXp3brn6N5CKUm_b79hNgAvIjNOwCUrpaQhVvOIYxrpQEFOY2_FA

[76] Loucks, E. B., Buka, S. L., Rogers, M. L., Liu, T., Kawachi, I., Kubzansky, L. D., Martin, L. T., & Gilman, S. E. (2012). Education and coronary heart disease risk associations may be affected by early-life common prior causes: a propensity matching analysis. *Ann Epidemiol*, *22*(4), 221-232. https://doi.org/10.1016/j.annepidem.2012.02.005

[77] Smith, K. J., & Victor, C. (2019). Typologies of loneliness, living alone and social isolation, and their associations with physical and mental health. *Ageing & Society*, *39*(8), 1709-1730. https://doi.org/10.1017/S0144686X18000132

[78] Gaggero, A., & Tommasi, D. (2020). Time of Day, Cognitive Tasks and Efficiency Gains. *SSRN Electronic Journal*. https://doi.org/10.2139/ssrn.3687134

[79] Hazelhoff, E. M., Dudink, J., Meijer, J. H., & Kervezee, L. (2021). Beginning to See the Light: Lessons Learned From the Development of the Circadian System for Optimizing Light Conditions in the Neonatal Intensive Care Unit. *Front Neurosci*, *15*, 634034. https://doi.org/10.3389/fnins.2021.634034

[80] Rauscher, F. G., Francke, M., Hiemisch, A., Kiess, W., & Michael, R. (2021). Ocular biometry in children and adolescents from 4 to 17 years: a cross-sectional study in central Germany. *Ophthalmic and Physiological Optics, 41*(3), 496-511. https://doi.org/https://doi.org/10.1111/opo.12814

[81] Zhang, J., & Deng, G. (2020). Protective effects of increased outdoor time against myopia: a review. *J Int Med Res, 48*(3), 300060519893866. https://doi.org/10.1177/0300060519893866

[82] Xiong, S., Sankaridurg, P., Naduvilath, T., Zang, J., Zou, H., Zhu, J., Lv, M., He, X., & Xu, X. (2017). Time spent in outdoor activities in relation to myopia prevention and control: a meta-analysis and systematic review. *Acta Ophthalmol, 95*(6), 551-566. https://doi.org/10.1111/aos.13403

[83] DeCarlo, D. K., Swanson, M., McGwin, G., Visscher, K., & Owsley, C. (2016). ADHD and Vision Problems in the National Survey of Children's Health. *Optom Vis Sci, 93*(5), 459-465. https://doi.org/10.1097/opx.0000000000000823

[84] Sherwin, J. C., Kokavec, J., & Thornton, S. N. (2015). Hydration, fluid regulation and the eye: in health and disease. *Clin Exp Ophthalmol, 43*(8), 749-764. https://doi.org/10.1111/ceo.12546

[85] MacGillivray, T. J., Trucco, E., Cameron, J. R., Dhillon, B., Houston, J. G., & van Beek, E. J. (2014). Retinal imaging as a source of biomarkers for diagnosis, characterization and prognosis of chronic illness or long-term conditions. *Br J Radiol, 87*(1040), 20130832. https://doi.org/10.1259/bjr.20130832

[86] Eto, T., & Higuchi, S. (2023). Review on age-related differences in non-visual effects of light: melatonin suppression, circadian phase shift and pupillary light reflex in children to older adults. *J Physiol Anthropol, 42*(1), 11. https://doi.org/10.1186/s40101-023-00328-1

[87] Fakorede, S. T., Akpan, L. G., Adekoya, K. O., & Oboh, B. (2022). Prevalence and population genetic data of colour vision deficiency among students from selected tertiary institutions in Lagos State, Nigeria. *Egyptian Journal of Medical Human Genetics, 23*(1), 73. https://doi.org/10.1186/s43042-022-00287-9

[88] Jordan, G., Deeb, S. S., Bosten, J. M., & Mollon, J. D. (2010). The dimensionality of color vision in carriers of anomalous trichromacy. *J Vis, 10*(8), 12. https://doi.org/10.1167/10.8.12

[89] de Gelder, B., Tamietto, M., van Boxtel, G., Goebel, R., Sahraie, A., van den Stock, J., Stienen, B. M. C., Weiskrantz, L., & Pegna, A. (2008). Intact navigation skills after bilateral loss of striate cortex. *Current Biology, 18*(24), R1128-R1129. https://doi.org/https://doi.org/10.1016/j.cub.2008.11.002

[90] Birch, E. E., & O'Connor, A. R. (2017). Chapter 72 - Binocular vision. In S. R. Lambert & C. J. Lyons (Eds.), *Taylor and Hoyt's Pediatric Ophthalmology and Strabismus (Fifth Edition)* (pp. 746-753.e742). Elsevier. https://doi.org/https://doi.org/10.1016/B978-0-7020-6616-0.00072-4

[91] Weger, U. W., & Inhoff, A. W. (2006). Attention and eye movements in reading: inhibition of return predicts the size of regressive saccades. *Psychol Sci, 17*(3), 187-191. https://doi.org/10.1111/j.1467-9280.2006.01683.x

92 Abusharha, A. A. (2017). Changes in blink rate and ocular symptoms during different reading tasks. *Clin Optom (Auckl)*, *9*, 133-138. https://doi.org/10.2147/opto.S142718

93 Mure, L. S. (2021). Intrinsically Photosensitive Retinal Ganglion Cells of the Human Retina [Review]. *Frontiers in Neurology, 12*. https://doi.org/10.3389/fneur.2021.636330

94 National Research Council (US) and Institute of Medicine (US) Committee on Integrating the Science of Early Childhood Development; Shonkoff JP, Phillips DA, editors. From Neurons to Neighborhoods: The Science of Early Childhood Development. Washington (DC): National Academies Press (US); 2000. 8, The Developing Brain. Available from: https://www.ncbi.nlm.nih.gov/books/NBK225562/

95 Munawar, K., Kuhn, S. K., & Haque, S. (2018). Understanding the reminiscence bump: A systematic review. *PLoS One*, *13*(12), e0208595. https://doi.org/10.1371/journal.pone.0208595

96 Balakrishnan, G., Uppinakudru, G., Girwar Singh, G., Bangera, S., Dutt Raghavendra, A., & Thangavel, D. (2014). A comparative study on visual choice reaction time for different colors in females. *Neurol Res Int, 2014*, 301473. https://doi.org/10.1155/2014/301473

97 Raju H, Tadi P. Neuroanatomy, Somatosensory Cortex. [Updated 2022 Nov 7]. In: StatPearls [Internet]. Treasure Island (FL): StatPearls Publishing; 2023 Jan-. Available from: https://www.ncbi.nlm.nih.gov/books/NBK555915/

98 Guarnera, M., Hichy, Z., Cascio, M. I., & Carrubba, S. (2015). Facial Expressions and Ability to Recognize Emotions From Eyes or Mouth in Children. *Eur J Psychol, 11*(2), 183-196. https://doi.org/10.5964/ejop.v11i2.890

99 Tsushima, Y., Okada, S., Kawai, Y., Sumita, A., Ando, H., & Miki, M. (2020). Effect of illumination on perceived temperature. *PLoS One, 15*(8), e0236321. https://doi.org/10.1371/journal.pone.0236321

[100] Kombeiz, O., Steidle, A., & Dietl, E. (2017). View it in a different light: Mediated and moderated effects of dim warm light on collaborative conflict resolution. *Journal of Environmental Psychology, 51*, 270-283.

[101] Ishikawa, A., & Kusumi, T. (2022). How do the Indoor Illumination Levels Affect Social and Cognitive Behaviors? *International Journal of Affective Engineering.*

[102] Biswas, D., Szocs, C., Chacko, R., & Wansink, B. (2017). Shining Light on Atmospherics: How Ambient Light Influences Food Choices. *Journal of Marketing Research, 54*(1), 111-123. https://doi.org/10.1509/jmr.14.0115

[103] Ru, T., Ma, Y., Zhong, L., Chen, Q., Ma, Y., & Zhou, G. (2022). Effects of Ambient Illuminance on Explicit and Implicit Altruism: The Mediation Roles of Perceived Anonymity and Satisfaction with Light. *Int J Environ Res Public Health, 19*(22). https://doi.org/10.3390/ijerph192215092

[104] Mehta, V., Mukherjee, S., & Manjaly, J. A. (2017). Can Lighting Influence Self-Disclosure? *Front Psychol*, *8*, 234. https://doi.org/10.3389/fpsyg.2017.00234

[105] Age of the property is the biggest single factor in energy efficiency of homes, Office for National Statistics Jan 2022, available at https://www.ons.gov.uk/peoplepopulationandcommunity/housing/articles/ageofthepropertyisthebiggestsinglefactorinenergyefficiencyofhomes/2021-11-01#:~:text=Homes%20in%20England%20and%20Wales%20were%20most%20commonly%20built%20between,and%20in%20Wales%2C%205%25 retrieved 4 July 2023

[106] Parental Spend Report GSK 2019, available at https://gkandpartners.com/parental-spend-report retrieved 4 July 2023

[107] Makaremi, N., Schiavoni, S., Pisello, A. L., & Cotana, F. (2019). Effects of surface reflectance and lighting design strategies on energy consumption and visual comfort. *Indoor and Built Environment, 28*(4), 552-563. https://doi.org/10.1177/1420326x18793170

[108] Tregenza, P., Stewart, L., & Sharples, S. (1999). Reduction of glazing transmittance by atmospheric pollutants. *Lighting Research & Technology - LIGHTING RES TECHNOL, 31*, 135-138. https://doi.org/10.1177/096032719903100401

[109] Housing Wire Blog 1 December 2021. How smart home technology increases property value in a challenging market https://www.housingwire.com/articles/how-smart-home-technology-increases-property-value-in-a-challenging-market/ retrieved 4 July 2023.